P9-CAL-594

Ten Things
I Learned Wrong
from a
Conservative
Church

Other Books by John Killinger

Lost in Wonder, Love, and Praise: Prayers and Affirmations for Christian Worship (Abingdon, 2001)

Preaching the New Millennium (Abingdon, 1999)

Raising Your Spiritual Awareness Through 365 Simple Gifts from God (Abingdon, 1998)

The Night Jessie Sang at the Opry (Angel Books, 1996)

Preaching to a Church in Crisis: A Homiletic for the Last Days of the Mainline Church (CSS, 1996)

Day by Day with Jesus: A Devotional Commentary on the Four Gospels (Abingdon, 1994)

Jessie: A Novel (McCracken, 1993)

Beginning Prayer (Upper Room, 1993)

Letting God Bless You: The Beatitudes for Today (Abingdon, 1992)

You Are What You Believe: The Apostles' Creed for Today (Abingdon, 1990)

Christmas Spoken Here (Broadman, 1989)

To My People with Love: The Ten Commandments for Today (Abingdon, 1988)

The God Named Hallowed: The Lord's Prayer for Today (Abingdon, 1987)

Christ and the Seasons of Marriage (Broadman, 1987)

Parables for Christmas (Abingdon, 1985)

Fundamentals of Preaching (Fortress, 1985; SCM, 1986; rev. 1998)

Christ in the Seasons of Ministry (Word, 1983)

The Loneliness of Children (Vanguard, 1980; Editions Robert Laffont, 1983)

His Power in You (Doubleday, 1978)

A Sense of His Presence (Doubleday, 1977)

Bread for the Wilderness, Wine for the Journey (Word, 1976)

The Salvation Tree (Harper & Row, 1973)

World in Collapse: The Vision of Absurd Drama (Dell, 1973)

The Fragile Presence: Transcendence in Contemporary Literature (Fortress, 1973)

Leave It to the Spirit: Freedom and Responsibility in the New Liturgies (Harper & Row, 1971)

For God's Sake, Be Human (Word, 1970)

The Failure of Theology in Modern Literature (Abingdon, 1965)

Hemingway and the Dead Gods (University Press of Kentucky, 1960; Citadel, 1965)

Ten Things
I Learned Wrong
from a
Conservative
Church

John Killinger

A Crossroad Carlisle Book
The Crossroad Publishing Company
New York • Berkeley

The Crossroad Publishing Company
481 Eighth Avenue, New York, NY 10001

Copyright © 2002 by John Killinger

All rights reserved. No part of this book may be reproduced, stored in a retrieval system, or transmitted, in any form or by any means, electronic, mechanical, photocopying, recording, or otherwise, without the written permission of The Crossroad Publishing Company.

Printed in the United States of America

Library of Congress Cataloging-in-Publication Data

Killinger, John.
    Ten things I learned wrong from a conservative church / John Killinger.
        p. cm.
    Includes bibliographical references.
    ISBN 0-8245-2011-4
    1. Fundamentalism. 2. Theology, Doctrinal – Popular works.
    3. Conservatism – Religious aspects – Christianity.   I. Title.
    BT82.2 .K53 2002
    230'.044 – dc21

                                        2002007790

1 2 3 4 5 6 7 8 9 10   08 07 06 05 04 03 02

For my dear friends
JERRY & SARAH WELBORN
who will not only forgive me for the opinions
expressed in this book
but probably arrived at many of them
before I did

Contents

Introduction

A conservative church probably saved my life. I want that understood. When I was an adolescent it changed my very existence, and I have always been grateful for that. It became my parent, my community, my lover. I expect my life would have been hell without it.

I loved my parents and still do, but our home was not always happy. My father, tall, slender, and good looking in his youth, conducted an extramarital affair for years. It made him feel guilty, and feeling guilty made him irritable and hard to live with. He was often frustrated and unhappy, which made him abusive. He bullied my mother and me unmercifully.

My sister, Nancy Jo, was killed by a runaway truck shortly before my twelfth birthday. I was like our mother, she resembled our father. Because of their connection, I think her death hurt my father irreparably. After she died, he tried insistently to divorce my mother, willing her to return to her father's home and me to go to military school. I hated the thought of military school. It was the sword of Damocles that hung for years over my young life.

I had three escapes. One was into the hills and creeks around the small farm where we lived a couple of miles from town. I spent most of my waking hours, when I wasn't in school or working, in the outdoors. The second was my drawing, painting, and lettering. Art appeared to be my primary talent, and I dreamed of making it a career. It was one thing about me of which my father seemed to approve. The third escape was the church, which had become important to me the year before my sister was killed.

My father had grown up in the Methodist church in Iowa, where his father was an elder. But something had turned my father off the church either before I was born or shortly thereafter, and he never attended. My mother was raised a Baptist, although she attended somewhat irregularly after we moved to the country, because she did not have a car and my father refused to take us. In decent weather, we sometimes walked the two miles to the Baptist church in Somerset, Kentucky, where we attended Sunday school.

It was on one of these occasional Sundays in my eleventh year that I heard a visiting evangelist, came under conviction, as they say, and gave my heart to Jesus. My mother was so proud the day I was baptized. For a long time after my sister's death, however, she did not feel like going to church regularly. I often went alone. We had gotten a new pastor shortly after my baptism, a tall, dignified, slightly portly man named Preston L. Ramsey, who surprised me by learning my name and taking an interest in me. Brother Ramsey, as most people called him, had not been to seminary, but he had been given an honorary doctorate from Union University in Tennessee and preferred to be called Doctor Ramsey.

I will always remember Dr. Ramsey as a great pastor. He truly cared about people — even agonized about them. Years later I would read Conrad Richter's novel *A Simple Honorable Man,* about a genuinely good man named Reverend Harry Donner, who ministered to a congregation in the Pennsylvania coal fields and sometimes prayed for hours over some of his suffering church members. When I read about Harry Donner, I thought of Preston Ramsey. I am sure he prayed for me, as he did for most of the people in his flock.

Two other people in First Baptist Church became very influential in my life. One was my Sunday school superintendent, a kind, elegant lady who was married to the owner of a local oil refinery. One day she and her husband, whose lovely home was halfway out the highway to my own home, stopped and offered me a ride. From then on, whenever they saw me standing around after church, they invited me to ride with them. Their car was a Cadillac — the only one in town — and I felt quite special arriving home in such a fine carriage.

The other person was Miss Lillian Vaughn, our church secretary. Miss Vaughn was only thirty-nine when she arrived at First Baptist Church, but she was already a confirmed spinster. She was as married to the church as any nun could ever be. Miss Vaughn genuinely loved everybody — even people who didn't like her, I'm convinced — and took a particular interest in the young people of her Training Union department, which I attended on Sunday evenings. Discovering my artistic ability, she began asking me to make posters and do other little jobs for her, always praising me scandalously for whatever I did. I was starved for acceptance, and I ate it up.

The miracle was that almost everybody in First Baptist Church treated me the way these three people did. When I rededicated my life to Christ at the age of fifteen, and then felt called to the ministry at sixteen, they were all so good to me that I felt embarrassed. If matters in my own home deteriorated, as they did until I left for college at seventeen, in the church they were always upbeat, warm, and accepting.

I was so encouraged by those generous people that I was actually happy. In my senior year of high school, I helped to form a new debate team, thinking the speaking experience would help prepare me for ministry. My partner and I began winning honors throughout the state. Church members belonging to various civic clubs invited me to speak for them, and treated me as handsomely as if I were a visiting dignitary. They all appeared to take pride in my calling to the ministry and stopped me on the streets in town to talk about it.

When I returned home from the university at Christmas, Dr. Ramsey asked me to preach at an evening service. Afterward, people shook my hand, hugged me, and promised that I was "going places." Some predicted I would be president of Southern Baptist Theological Seminary. One couple, more widely traveled, said I would be minister of Riverside Church or president of Union Theological Seminary in New York. It was heady stuff for a shy, introspective boy who had never appeared to fit in anywhere.

This supportive adoration continued through the years of my education and through all my incarnations as a minister and teacher. In 1999, I returned as one of the preachers for First Baptist Church's two-hundredth anniversary, and found that many of the folks who had been there when I was a boy were just as kind and encouraging as they had ever been. And even some people who had joined the congregation since I left said they had heard about me and were very happy to have me there to speak.

It should be easy for the reader to see, therefore, that my life has been profoundly changed by that church. I can easily say that I wouldn't be the person I am today — for whatever that's worth — if it had not been for the love and encouragement of that wonderful congregation. And as I am very happy with my life today, and with my feelings about God and my whole existence, I shall be forever grateful to those people for their unfailing support and affection. They helped to bring me to this point, and I am keenly aware of my great debt to them.

Now, ALL OF THAT BEING SAID, I should perhaps draw a line here across the entire page to indicate that there is another side of the coin. What I am going to say is in no way a criticism of the dear folks who have always meant so much to me, still do, and always will. It is simply a collection of observations about life and theology as I now understand them, and how the life and theology I now understand actually differ from the things I learned, almost uncritically, as a young man in the Baptist church.

Even as a young man, I was not totally without analytical faculties. Dr. Ramsey was extremely tolerant of me. I loved to go to his home, often in the evening or on a Sunday afternoon, and discuss something he had said in a sermon or some bit of information I had come across in a book. I realize now what an imposition this must have been on his kindly nature, and how often I intruded on him and his wife at times that should have been theirs alone. But Dr. Ramsey was fond of argument, and we frequently took differing positions in our discussions, even though I hardly knew enough to defend any point of view at all.

On the whole, however, I accepted without reservation the Baptist church's position on most moral and doctrinal issues, and carried them about for years as the foundation of my philosophical outlook. Even during my time at Harvard University's Divinity School, when I was encountering "heretical" ideas and opinions as thick as fireflies on a June night, I held consistently to my Baptist heritage, while memorizing the positions of our "enemies," trying to understand how anyone could possibly come to such erroneous or absurd conclusions.

I cannot say, in fact, when my confidence in this heritage began to erode, and when I started to develop in my own direction toward the person I am today. I still considered myself very much a Baptist after graduating from Harvard, as well as a few years later when I graduated from Princeton Theological Seminary with a doctor of theology degree, and finally when I became academic dean of a Baptist college in Louisville, Kentucky, now part of the University of Louisville. And I thought I was a faithful Baptist in 1966 when I flew out to Mill Valley, California, to address a student mission conference at Golden Gate Baptist Theological Seminary and subsequently found myself targeted by the president of that seminary and by the executive secretary of the Southern Baptist Convention for ideas at variance with theirs, particularly about our denomination and what I perceived as its phobia about new ideas and freedom of expression.

Sometime between leaving Somerset, Kentucky, to go to college, and that unnerving experience with the Southern Baptist hierarchy, I had apparently begun to reconsider vital sections of the theology I imbibed as a boy. I was still not really conscious of this and assumed that others were out of sync with Baptist teachings, not me. I really wanted to remain a Baptist and was prepared to hammer out any solutions necessary to do so. I was like Carlyle Marney, the minister of the elegant Myers Park Baptist Church in Charlotte, North Carolina, who when asked once by a college coed, "Dr. Marney, since you're so critical of the Baptist church, why don't you go somewhere else?" ingratiatingly replied, "Honey, where else is there?" I had never considered going anyplace else. The Baptist church was my home, my family, my be-all and end-all — or so I thought at the time.

There is no reason the reader should be aware of my pilgrimage in the decades since I met such static at Golden Gate, so I should briefly rehearse it. At the time of that unhappy experience, I had gone as a young professor of preaching, worship, and literature to Vanderbilt Divinity School in Nashville, where I remained for fifteen years. Dr. James L. Sullivan, who was then the executive secretary of the Southern Baptist Convention, telephoned Dr. Rob Roy Purdy, the vice-chancellor of Vanderbilt, to insist that I should be dismissed for what I had said at Golden Gate. Dr. Purdy, bless his heart, replied, "You may do that sort of thing in Baptist institutions, Mr. Sullivan, but we don't do it at Vanderbilt." Vanderbilt was a nurturing habitat for me during those fifteen years, and I have always been grateful for a place where I could earn my living while thinking about the most important things in life and enjoying my wife and two young sons to an almost inordinate degree.

Returning at midlife to a desire to fulfill my ministry calling, I spent a year actively seeking a parish to serve. Among the churches where I interviewed was a Baptist church in Houston, Texas, known as a moderate church. But when I learned that they had rejected one candidate for saying he wasn't sure about the virgin birth of Jesus, I knew I would not be comfortable as the minister of that church, even though I could honestly say I had no problem with the traditional teaching about the virgin birth. With two invitations in hand, one from the First Presbyterian Church in Lynchburg, Virginia, and the other from the First Congregational Church of Los Angeles, California, I accepted the call from Lynchburg, for the church there appeared to me stronger and under better discipline than the other, and I believed, as one just leaving the ivory tower of seminary teaching, I would be better suited to be the pastor of that church. It was simply "safer." The folks in California were very understanding. "We'll hire an older minister," they said, "and when he retires, we'll call again."

If I thought the time in Lynchburg would be idyllic, with plenty of ease in which to sharpen my gifts as a parish minister, I was wrong. I had been there only a few months when I inadvertently provoked a war with the Rev. Jerry Falwell, minister of the Thomas Road Baptist Church, preacher on the Old-Time Gospel Hour, and head of the Moral Majority, all three of which were centered in Lynchburg. The war began over some remarks I made about the Falwell ministry's style of Christianity, not with the intention of criticizing Falwell but with the aim of setting up my own congregation for a review of its approach to ministry. I did not know Falwell would hear what I said and take umbrage at it.

Perhaps it was during my six years in Lynchburg that I realized most clearly how "un-Baptist" I was becoming, for if Falwell claimed to represent the "correct" Baptist point of view, then I could hardly claim fidelity to the same set of beliefs. As a pastor, I found that I was still very much the teacher, desiring to impart information and understanding to my parishioners. I often preached series of sermons, not just individual ones, on such vital Christian subjects as the Lord's Prayer, the Ten Commandments, and the nature of the Bible. Inasmuch as I was conducting this kind of teaching ministry in the shadow of the Falwell empire, more powerful then than it is today, I attempted to think my way through a lot of ideas and issues with a freshness and creativity that invariably led me to question a number of things in my own Baptist background.

The people at First Congregational Church in Los Angeles were as good as their word. The Sunday afternoon following their minister's announcement of his retirement, I received a telephone call asking if I would again consider coming as their minister. I said I would, and a few months later we were packing to move to the West Coast.

If Lynchburg, Virginia, had been a place of great theological precision, where religious views were stated plainly and forcefully, Los Angeles was just the opposite. In a sprawling metropolis of widely varied views and nonviews, the congregation I served appeared to understand almost nothing of traditional Christian belief — and not to care. Challenged by this great cotton-candy approach to everything, I tried to impart some theological structure to our congregational life and understanding by preaching sermons on basic Christian beliefs, including a series on the Apostles' Creed.

By this time, in the late 1980s, I surely knew what I believed as a Christian and understood that it differed in some significant ways from the things I had learned as a young man in the First Baptist Church of Somerset, Kentucky. I was still very grateful for the experiences I had enjoyed there, and especially for the discipline of Bible study from my Baptist background, for I regarded the lack of biblical knowledge as one of the biggest limitations in the life of my new congregation. But I was beginning to see quite clearly that many of the things I had been taught and accepted without question either did not fit well with my personal experience, or failed to satisfy the tests of consistency and congruency I now applied to most theological concepts.

The key issue, I realized again as I had in my contest with Jerry Falwell, was the nature of the Bible and biblical authority. If one could assume the inerrancy of every word and teaching in the Bible, then one might construct a doctrinal edifice on that foundation which would withstand all criticism, regardless of how incompatible with other realities it might appear. But if one could not assume this, then one must rely much more heavily on human reason and experience to establish the tenets of one's thought and understanding. In retrospect, my years as a graduate student in English and American literature made me too critical of textual matters to accept the inerrancy of the Scriptures so easily. I had in fact during those years written a long poem about faith that included this quatrain about biblical literalism:

> But what of poor Lucan who erred as a scribe
> When his wandering eye on Lucia lit?
> And what of the poor little purgativ'd fly
> Who added his bit to holy writ?

When I received an invitation in 1989 to become Distinguished Professor of Religion and Culture at Samford University in Birmingham, Alabama, with the opportunity to be part of a new divinity school being established there, it seemed a wonderful time to bid adieu to the parish, return to academia, and try to consolidate my thoughts and experiences of a lifetime in religious settings. That, alas, was not to be. I had barely arrived on the Samford campus when I became aware of how much my presence was resented by a certain administrator because I represented a freer, more open approach to religious truth than his ideology could tolerate.

In the winter and spring of 1992–93, while I was on a six-month sabbatical leave at Oxford University in England, Jerry Falwell came to the Samford campus to speak at the Cumberland School of Law. When someone asked him about me, he remarked that I should not be allowed to teach on a Christian campus like Samford's. I returned to Birmingham in June to find that the dean of the divinity school had ordered my name and courses stricken from the school's computers.

The break was complete. I had tried to return to the circle of Baptist life and to spend my remaining years sharing with Baptist students some of what I had gleaned in my years of teaching and ministry. Now, while the university administration was willing for me to remain and teach undergraduates in the departments of English and religion, I found it impossible to continue on the campus.

After leaving Samford in 1996, I became president of a nonprofit international organization called the Mission for Biblical Literacy, which supports the reading of the Scriptures without any particular theological bias, and remained in that office until 2001. I also began to spend my summers as minister of the Little Stone Church, a resort congregation on Mackinac Island, Michigan. I continue to write and publish books and to reflect on where my journey in ministry has carried me over the years. Writing helps to clarify the mind. It probably does more for the writer than for the reader. And this is undoubtedly the reason it occurred to me to write this particular book.

I do not write out of any spirit of spite or revenge. As I said at the outset, I love my heritage in the conservative branch of the church and credit it with a great deal of the joy and happiness I feel with my life experiences. No, I set down these chapters as a record of how my mind has changed across the years, of the way certain fundamental teachings that once formed the basis of my wisdom and understanding have shifted. It may well be that some of my readers are in the process of analyzing the teachings they have received in the light of their own experiences, and that my reflections may assist them in their reflection.

While the world may not be greatly affected by what we think or believe as individuals, our own destinies are certainly altered by it. It is therefore very important to struggle to clarify our thoughts and beliefs continuously throughout our lives. If we are serious about reexamining everything all the time, we shall go through many transformations in a lifetime.

One of the guiding images of my life, since I first read it a quarter of a century ago in Sir Francis Chichester's *The Lonely Sea and the Sky,* has been the picture of Chichester, the intrepid explorer, piloting his tiny aircraft in the first solo flight across the Tasmanian Sea, between New Zealand and Australia. Even though the plane was equipped with extra fuel tanks, Chichester still had to set it down en route for refueling. He had selected tiny Falkland Island as the place to do this — a diminutive strip of land approximately halfway between his take-off point and destination. His flight commenced on a clear, sunny day. But before he had gone far, clouds covered the sky and winds buffeted his small plane, driving it off course.

Eventually, in the distance, Chichester saw a break in the clouds. Abandoning his course, he headed for the break. Once there, he held the throttle between his knees as he made calculations with his sextant. Replotting his course, he set out again, in precisely the right direction, he hoped, for Falkland Island. It was a very risky business, for if he missed his objective he would crash in the sea without the possibility of rescue.

The same thing happened repeatedly. Again and again, the plane was blown off course. Each time, Chichester patiently waited for the sun to break through somewhere, then diverted his plane to the spot and took new readings. It seemed almost a miracle when he finally took his plane down through the clouds and beheld the small island, green and welcoming, before him.

Is there a more apt analogy for our lives? Some days are bright and sunny, and we have no trouble at all staying on course. Then the storms come, and we are swept this way and that. Sometimes our objectives appear completely lost to us. But we take new readings from such light as we get, and reset our courses for the precious destination.

This is the way we work out what we believe about everything. Do you remember what Frederick Buechner said in *The Alphabet of Grace?*

> At its heart most theology, like most fiction, is essentially autobiography. Aquinas, Calvin, Barth, Tillich, working out their systems in their own ways and in their own language, are all telling us the stories of their lives, and if you press them far enough, even at their most cerebral and forbidding, you find an experience of flesh and blood, a human face smiling or weeping or covering its eyes before something that happened once. What happened once may be no more than a child falling sick, a thunderstorm, a dream, and yet it made for the face and inside the face a difference which no theology can ever entirely convey or entirely conceal.[1]

The stuff of our lives *must* be interwoven with what we believe, must test it and twist it and prove it a thousand times. Otherwise we have not lived, and our theology is nothing more than a fairy tale.

First Wrong Teaching

The Bible Is the Literal, Inerrant Word of God

My first Bible was a Christmas gift from the sister I lost when she was nine and I was almost twelve. It was the Authorized or King James Version, of course, one of the most felicitous translations ever made, at least from a lilting, rhetorical point of view. From the day I became a Christian I began to read it, usually at night, in my little attic space of a room. My parents' house was small, with only two tiny bedrooms. My father occupied one, and my mother and sister the other. I was assigned to the attic, which because there was no wallboarding or insulation, was extremely cold in winter and hot in summer. But I was happy, in spite of this, to have my own space where I could be alone to read and pray and dream. The space contained a small bed, an old rocking chair that had once resided in our living room, and a small army-surplus cardboard filing case, in which I kept pen and paper, my Bible, and a few other books. The only reading lamp was the naked light bulb at the ceiling, switched on by pulling a string. I usually sat on my bed to read, unless it was too cold, and then pulled the string and knelt by the bed to pray.

That Bible was sacred to me. Not only because my sister had given it to me, but because our pastor had assured me it was the very Word of God — every word that was in it. He was fond of quoting 2 Timothy 3:16, "All Scripture is given by inspiration of God, and is profitable for doctrine,

13

for reproof, for correction, for instruction in righteousness."
He also liked to cite Revelation 22:18–19: "If any man shall
add unto these things, God shall add unto him the plagues
that are written in this book; and if any man shall take away
from the words of the book of this prophecy, God shall take
away his part out of the book of life, and out of the holy city,
and from the things which are written in this book."

Not once can I recall the minister's having explained to
the congregation that the Bible was a compendium of individual writings assembled by the church by the end of the
second century A.D. to combat the rash teachings of a man
named Marcion, who found such incompatibility between
the judgmental, warlike God of the Hebrew Scriptures and
the loving, generous God of the Christian experience that
he wanted to abandon the former and cleave only to the writings of early Christians. To have done so would have thrown
an entirely different light on the solemn curse at the end
of Revelation, causing it to refer to the strange, prophetic
Book of Revelation alone and not to the entire Bible as we
have come to know it.

My reading in those days, as well as I can remember, was
primarily in Genesis, Exodus, Psalms, some of the prophets,
and the Gospels and Pauline writings in the New Testament.
I am sure I found the minutiae of the legal system in Leviticus rather strange and foreign, if I read Leviticus at all, and
the Song of Solomon unconvincing for a lad still in very early
adolescence. But I loved the Psalms and the Gospels, and
was often transported in reading them from my plain surroundings to the romantic hills and busy pathways of early
Palestine. I knew the geography of those faint-colored maps
in the back of my Bible better than I did that of the U.S. or
even my own state of Kentucky.

And much as I wanted to mark certain ringing passages
I came across in the Bible — either for their own beauty or
for the way they spoke to my lonely, hungry heart — I never

did, for I regarded that book as too holy for my inscriptions. I did not exactly *fear* to do it, as if I might be struck dead or visited by an illness if I did. Yet I did too fear it, in the same way that one is said to fear the Lord — to have such dreadful respect for holiness that one forebears crossing a certain threshold between the human and divine.

I have read of a certain tribe in Africa which regards a particular lake as the residence of their deity. When the men of the tribe go on a fishing expedition on the lake, therefore, they tie cloths around their oars to muffle the sounds, lest they offend the deity by their clumsy approach.

This was the way I felt about not making marks in my Bible. It was so holy, so redolent of the divine spirit, that I regarded it with an almost agonizing humility. I sometimes think of this now — and especially did when I was teaching courses in the Bible at Samford University — for my present favorite copy of the Bible, an NRSV given me by my minister son, is so heavily underlined and bracketed in places that it's hard to read. I have come a long way from those early days of wonder and trepidation, but I greatly cherish the memory of them. I'm *glad* I began by thinking the Bible a holy book, and that I have recollections of the sense of *sanctum sanctorum* I felt when I approached the reading of it. The Bible is so special, so filled with the records of people's encounters with God, that it ought to feel holy. It ought to inspire us with dread and awe as we open its covers and are confronted by the extraordinary things it has to say.

The appearance of the Revised Standard Version of the Bible in 1952 (the RSV New Testament had appeared six years earlier) was largely a nonoccasion for me. It was the year of my courtship and marriage. I was pastoring a rural church on the weekends and going to college during the week. And after we married, my wife and I packed all our belongings into the back of a 1940 Ford and set out for Texas, more than a thousand miles from home, where I completed my degree at Baylor University. Since then, I have heard scholars on the RSV committee tell hair-raising tales of the demonstrations they witnessed, the letters they received, and the threats made against their lives. I vaguely remember the book-burnings, especially in Southern Baptist churches, and I have images in my mind of hooded Ku Klux Klan members gathering in woodsy places to consign copies of the new Bible to raging bonfires.

The hullaballoo was mainly over a verse in Isaiah in which the King James translators had spoken of a "virgin" who would conceive and bear a child, while the modern translation, following more reliable manuscripts, spoke of a "young woman." The witching wands of the heresy detectives immediately signaled an attack on the virginity of Mary, the mother of Jesus, and hurled their holy invective at the translation and the translators alike.

I suspected then, and still do, that much of the conflict was political in nature, not really spiritual or doctrinal. Of all the significant denominations in the U.S. opposed to the National Council of Churches, which sponsored the new translation, none was more vehement or outspoken than the Southern Baptist Convention. So when the NCC's Bible appeared, the preachers most wont to criticize the organization were also the first to complain about the Bible it produced.

I think the fact that I was not disturbed about the re-translation of the reference to the young woman in Isaiah is a reliable guide to the way my mind was changing about the Bible. I believed then, and still do, that God rises above the Bible so majestically and transcendently that whatever happens to the Bible in its various translations and paraphrases is not likely to have much effect on him. In one of his books, my friend and mentor Paul E. Scherer described a quiet countryside in France during World War I. Suddenly the stillness was rent by the sound of a shell whistling through the air, and then by the deafening noise of an explosion. The birds along the front, accustomed to the behavior of bombs and shells, had risen high into the sky before human ears could even detect the approach of the shell. When the noise abated and the debris settled, the birds blithely descended to earth and went on about their business as before. This, I have long believed, is the way it is with God and the silly quarrels of human beings about doctrine or Bible translations or liturgical practices: he merely rises above them until they are over, then resettles himself as before, all but oblivious of our earnest conflict.

When I went to divinity school at Harvard, I studied with some of the finest biblical scholars in the modern world — Amos Wilder, Krister Stendal, Robert Pfeiffer, Frank Cross, Jr., and George Ernest Wright, among others. Stendal made us memorize the forbidding list of symbols in the Nestle and Hort Greek edition of the New Testament — the keys to all the ancient manuscripts consulted in hammering out a masterful text of the New Testament as it might have been in its earliest version. I found it dreadfully boring, for working on ancient manuscripts was not the sort of thing I ever wanted to do. I was not even excited by the discovery of the so-called Dead Sea Scrolls, for I could not envision their adding much to the story already told in present translations of the Scriptures.

The human stories of how the scrolls got there, probably in some ancient Essene community, how they were found by a shepherd boy who stumbled into the cave, how they were then bartered among dealers and scholars, and how various professors on the world scene, Frank Cross, Jr. and George Ernest Wright among them, were jockeying for control of the scrolls like a bunch of mafia members trying to shut out rival gangs, were more absorbing than the fact of the scrolls themselves, which have since confirmed information we already had about certain biblical manuscripts but, with one or two exceptions like the Gospel of Thomas, have added little that is new to our knowledge of God or the Bible.

What I have seen is a kind of literalism at work on both ends of the scholarly spectrum — among the religious conservatives on one end, who insist so stridently on a literal interpretation of the Scriptures as God's carefully dictated word, and on the other end the vast array of biblical academicians, who go to battle continuously over the supremacy of a particular manuscript or the parsing of a particular verb in the manuscript. I do not mean to denigrate either set of concerns. Yet I cannot help seeing something innately comical in their complementary enterprises that springs out of too serious a regard for the text itself, when the real object of their regard ought to be the sense of a divine presence that springs as surely from the text as the presence of Lincoln or Grant or Theodore Roosevelt leaps forth from a letter by them or their contemporaries.

I once heard the renowned fundamentalist Dr. Hagen Staack describe the action of one of his cherished professors in the Netherlands. The professor, he said, invariably began his work with a new class of Bible students each term by throwing his Bible onto the floor and leaping up and down on it with both feet. Then he explained to the students that he really held the Bible in the highest esteem, but behaved as he did because he wanted to demonstrate in some unforgettable manner that he really worshiped God, not the Bible.

That is a terribly vital distinction, it seems to me, and one that my pastor and others in the Baptist church never spoke about. I would have found such a gesture extremely helpful during the formative years, when I was trying to understand what it was that was so magical about the Scriptures. It was not the book itself; it was the God of whom the book speaks, and whose encounters with human beings are so wonderfully captured and rendered by the writers of the book.

IN 1970, WORD BOOKS, then located in Waco, Texas, and presided over by its courtly and gracious founder, Jarrell McCracken, published my little book *For God's Sake, Be Human.* I had written the book originally as a series of Sunday morning lectures for a class at the American Church in Paris, where I served in 1967–68 as theologian-in-residence. The class that heard the lectures was unique, if not in the intimidating mental prowess of its participants, then in the variety of their backgrounds, which included European representatives of many U.S. companies, and their spouses, plus a number of business people from other countries, several French citizens, and some American expatriates living in Paris.

I tried in the lectures to provide a stimulating recital of Christian theology, much of it personal and anecdotal, with the aim of provoking the liveliest discussion possible. It was my habit, then, to reflect on our discussions and rewrite the lectures on Monday morning, trying to incorporate insights from the discussants and to answer queries they had raised, especially those I considered representative of more widespread questioning. Often I would begin the lecture on a subsequent Sunday morning by recapping what had been said the week before and commenting on some thought that had occurred to me as a result of something one of the participants had said.

Because the thrust of the lectures was an attempt to examine the human side of spirituality, and to see what it means to be natural before God, I entitled the lecture on the Bible and the nature of biblical authority "The Human Depths of the Scriptures." In this lecture I argued that the Bible should not be discarded in our time as an arcane book about a Middle Eastern divinity, but should be seen as a dynamic record of countless people over a span of thousands of years trying to break through the veil of mystery and comprehend enough of the being of God to reorient their lives and reposition their culture. The Bible's authority, I suggested, rests in the very ingenuity and irresistibility of the experiences it describes, not in its having God as its author.

This was the first time I had really tried to make a statement about what I had come to understand about the Scriptures. As I said, it grew out of a larger attempt to create a kind of popular anthropology of our faith. Looking back now, I realize why I was coming to this view. As a professor of preaching eager to help my students make sense when they talked from the pulpit, I was struggling for an understanding of the Bible that would make it more preachable in our time. I wanted my students to make meaningful contact with the hearts and minds of their hearers, not merely announce in their presence the mandates of an irreproachable book from antiquity.

I was not really prepared for what happened after publication of the book. The Reverend Billy Graham, all-time dean of American evangelists, did not like what I had written about the Bible. That was his prerogative; I often find things I don't like in books. But Graham spoke to Jarrell McCracken and demanded that he withdraw my book from publication. If he didn't, said Graham, the powerful Christian Booksellers Association would boycott Word's publications.

I did not know this at the time. It was later confided to me by Ronald Patterson, then associate editor at Word and subsequently editor-in-chief at Abingdon Press in Nashville, with whom I also published. If I had admired Jarrell before hearing this story, I admired him doubly afterward, for he refused to take *For God's Sake, Be Human* out of circulation. Patterson said the CBA had indeed carried out Graham's threat to boycott Word, except for J. Keith Miller's *The Taste of New Wine,* which was selling so well that CBA dealers would not remove it from their shelves.

What Billy Graham did served more than ever to catalyze my thinking about the Bible and why conservatives are so dependent on a literalist view of the Scriptures. Over against Roman Catholicism, which has an authoritarian view of the church, many Protestants developed an authoritarian approach to the Bible itself. Among certain Protestant groups, this eventually amounted to actual biblicism, or idolatry of the text itself. Graham's aggressive action in behalf of a literal Bible, it seemed to me, represented an almost pathological view of the Scriptures.

"CREDO QUIA ABSURDUM EST," said one of the church fathers — "I believe because it is absurd." That is a noble statement when it comes to having faith in God despite a prevailing countermood in one's culture. Yet people put themselves in an unnecessary bind when they insist on the absolute, literal truth of the Scriptures. It means they forswear all human knowledge that doesn't agree with the Scriptures, including the evidence that the earth is round, not square, and must perform a lot of mental gymnastics to defend obvious textual differences within the Bible itself.

W. A. Criswell, longtime pastor of the First Baptist Church of Dallas, Texas, and once president of the Southern Baptist Convention, wrote a book called *Why I Preach That the Bible Is Literally True.* In it he insisted that "difficulties in the Scriptures do not overthrow their infallible nature," and that all the difficulties are merely "mountains yet to be scaled and lands yet to be conquered."[2] That is, when we know enough, we'll understand that none of the apparently erroneous statements in the Bible is really in error.

Criswell even tried to persuade his readers that the Bible is not many books but a single book, with God as its solitary author. It is a miraculous book, he said, because God made it that way. Sometimes his posturing is almost incredible, as in this excerpt:

> As I hold in my hands a copy of the divine, infallible, inerrant Word of God, I cannot but be overwhelmed by its miraculous preservation. Word for word, jot for jot, tittle for tittle, through the centuries, the saints possessed God's holy self-disclosure of himself. We, too, can be assured that the Bible we hold in our hands is the Word of God as the Lord wrote it, and that it contains what God would have in it, and that it does not contain what God refuses to make a part of it.[3]

Fundamentalists prefer such rhetoric to any serious wrestling with the problems in the biblical text, as I learned in my first encounter with Jerry Falwell. One of my well-meaning church members in Lynchburg, who happened to be an ardent fan of Falwell's, asked us both to lunch in his home. During the table conversation, I asked Falwell why he and other conservatives did not regard those of us with differing views of the Scriptures as Christians. "We accept you as brothers and sisters in Christ," I said. "Why don't you accord us the same courtesy?"

"That's a slippery slope," said Falwell. It was the first time I had heard that expression, but I was to hear it often in subsequent years. It is often used in debate to indicate that one must be careful when descending by a slippery path, for there may be no way of stopping. If Falwell and the conservatives accorded those holding other views of the Bible genuine Christian status, there might not be a convenient place for drawing a line of distinction between themselves and others.

"Then, Jerry," I said, "let me put another question to you. You are familiar with the four Gospels. You must know that in the Fourth Gospel, Jesus' cleansing of the temple comes very early, in only the second chapter, and is seen as a sort of grand act by which Jesus commenced his ministry. In the other Gospels, the synoptics, that same act is set at the end of Jesus' ministry, during the final week of his life. If the Bible is literally true and God inspired the writing of every word of it, as you claim, how do you account for that discrepancy? Was God being forgetful when he dictated the Fourth Gospel?"

Falwell cleared his throat and took a drink of iced tea.

"When I was a student at the Baptist Bible College of Missouri," he then said very matter-of-factly, "I had a professor who explained that all very well to my satisfaction."

Period.

That was all he would say on the matter. I don't know if he had forgotten the explanation or lacked the courage to undertake it for me. But that was it. It had been explained to him, and he was satisfied. *Credo quia absurdum est.*

How much richer the Bible is, in my estimation, when we allow it to be imperfect, a flawed record of people's intimations of immortality, their chance encounters with God, their earnest search for the meaning of life and the presence of the holy. God doesn't need an infallible Bible, and neither do we. It is better for us to interact fully with the Scriptures — to question and criticize, debate and interpret, scrutinize and analyze. Otherwise, we demean our own humanity and make ourselves as infantile and fanciful as children who imagine they have found a magic stone or the key to a secret passage.

Most of us do our own reasoning and testing of the Scriptures without even being aware of it. I remember a wonderful story by Walter Harrelson, one of the preeminent biblical scholars of our time and one of the preparers of the New Revised Standard Version of the Bible. Harrelson says that the first person to introduce him to the critical study of the Bible was his Aunt Zora, who instructed a class of boys in a country church in North Carolina. Aunt Zora loved the Bible and taught it with relish. But every once in a while, when she had finished reading a story in the Old Testament in which God had insisted on particularly cruel treatment of Israel's enemies, say the Canaanites or the Midianites, she would say, "Well, children, that's what the Bible says, and it must be true. But you know, there's something wrong somewhere, because God is not like that."

"The Bible itself," says Harrelson, "led Aunt Zora to a recognition that the biblical writers, who faithfully prepared the record of God's sacred teachings and saving deeds, sometimes must have misunderstood or slipped. God *could not have* commanded the Israelites to exterminate the entire population of Canaanites or the wives and children of the Midianites who had led Israel into apostasy. Why? Because that is untrue to the character of the God of the Bible."[4]

THE FACT IS that we do not have one single, solitary original manuscript of the Bible, from either the Old Testament or the New Testament, and that among the numerous extant manuscripts we do have, all copies of copies, there are so many differences of lettering or wording that enormous scholarship and patience are required to try to collate them into a reasonably accurate rendering of what the first writers of the books of the Bible intended. Even then, we are left with vast uncertainty about certain passages.

Wouldn't it be reasonable to expect that a God who troubled to dictate the Bible word for word to all the scribes who were involved in writing it would also have exerted the energy to protect the original manuscripts those scribes produced? Wouldn't he lead some Middle Eastern shepherd boy to stumble upon a cave where the original scrolls of the Book of Job and the Book of Genesis are preserved in pristine condition? Given the importance of Jesus and his mission to save the world, wouldn't God have insured the existence of the original four Gospels, or at least of one of them? If God meant for the Book of Revelation to be a program for the end of the world, wouldn't he have guaranteed the preservation of the original manuscript until at least the third or fourth century A.D.?

This is not a humorous matter. On the contrary, it is all extremely important. Our very disposition as Christians may well depend on how we regard the Bible. If we think of it as the completely literal, inerrant word of God, then we will read it as a talisman, as a mandate to do exactly as it says, even in the legalistic sections of the Torah. But if we see it as an extraordinary compilation of religious manuscripts, uneven in character, which nevertheless extol the majesty of God and invite us to journey with him in discovering what our world is like and how we can best devote ourselves to his service, then we shall be free to grow and grow and grow, and to continue to produce literature reflecting the rich exchange between the human and the divine.

THAT IS ANOTHER THING involved in the outcome of this debate over the nature of the Scriptures. If we regard the Bible as somehow magical, fixed, the authentic, final answer of God to everything, then every other piece of literature in the world is somehow inferior to it and cannot contain the intensity of holy presence we find there. But if on the other hand we look at the Bible as part of the sacred journey of human existence, an unusually glowing and intensive part, but only a part in spite of that, then we are instantly reminded that other literature can also reveal God and invite us into deeper relationship with him.

I cannot begin to name all the wonderful books that have bidden my soul to greater devotion toward God, much less the countless articles and notes that have evoked a sense of holiness when I read them. I think, for example, of the novels of British writers Miss Read (the pseudonym of Dora Saint) and Elizabeth Goudge, which so appreciate the glittering quality of the world around them, animate and inanimate, that they never fail to invoke in me a spirit of wonder and gratitude. Or the writings of Nikos Kazantzakis, rambunctious with life and brimming with vitality, whether he is writing about St. Francis of Assisi or Zorba the Greek or his own extremely colorful pilgrimage from Crete to Paris and Germany and back to Greece. Or the haunting volumes of Loren Eiseley, the anthropologist, who wrote so beautifully of the human story and often interspersed in his accounts the narrative of his own life, trembling with sensitivity for our short time on the earth and the sacredness of the various evidences we leave behind. Or Harry Williams's marvelous autobiography *Some Day I'll Find You,* with its numerous descriptions of epiphanies Williams has enjoyed since he first had a nervous breakdown and then became a whole person, both sadder and wiser and more worshipful. Or Michael Mayne's *This Sunrise of Wonder: Letters for the Journey,* every page of which is packed with insights and inspirations. It is a veritable cornucopia of poetic and informative delights.

I have a minister son whose early education was much superior to mine, and who has continued over the years to build on it with meticulous care, reading poets and philosophers I have never had the time or inclination to know. His list of special books would be so much longer and more refined than mine, and would probably begin with the German poet Rainer Maria Rilke, who has been as constant a source of inspiration to him as Kazantzakis or Mayne has been to me. My son loves the Bible too, and reads it with a critical facility far vaster than mine. What a loss it would be if he had felt such unshakeable loyalty to the Scriptures that he had not read beyond them, had not experienced the presence of God in more varied contemporary works!

There is the point, you see. A proper view of the Scriptures does not lead to an either/or position, able to find God in the Bible but nowhere else, or at least not so strongly and palpably in other places. It does not teach us to shy from the world of art and letters, philosophy and mathematics, science and technology, but to thrive in it, and to pursue the knowledge of God in all these areas, confident that the God who could create a world can continue to reveal himself in every facet of that world, through every vessel who loves and appreciates it, and even some who don't.

ONE OF THE ODDITIES of religious life in our time has been the devotion Billy Graham has shown toward the Living Bible, a paraphrase of the Scriptures published by Tyndale House Publishers of Wheaton, Illinois. The author of the paraphrase, Kenneth Taylor, said he began rewording the Bible for his children during his daily commutes to work so that the children could understand it. A paraphrase is very different from a translation. It is a free and easy recasting of the text in contemporary idiomatic speech, with more emphasis on communication than accuracy. I do not mean to imply that a paraphrase invariably strays from the meaning of the text, but it can easily put a "spin" on a text to make it support the author's particular theology or worldview in a subject, say, like eschatology.

The odd or ironic thing of which I speak is for Graham, who has been such an advocate of the literal, inerrant Scriptures, to promote a version of the Scriptures whose accuracy quotient would rank far below that of any other version, even the Authorized or King James Version of 1611. The image many of us have of Graham is of the tall, roughly handsome evangelist, tanned from hours on the golf course, holding aloft a large, limp-covered Bible as he quotes from it or preaches a sermon sprinkled with numerous directives beginning "The Lord says." According to his theology, the preacher must preach the word of God from the written text that is the very Word of God. But how does one do this from a Bible that is only a paraphrase, a loose rendering of a translation, whose aim is to create a gist of the text without even attempting to establish what that text might actually have said in the oldest manuscripts available?

I think this means that Graham has had two standards about the Bible. One is the old fundamentalist standard that insists on the literal inspiration of the Scriptures and the infallibility of holy text. The other, as Graham's understanding moderated because he was traveling the world and encountering other opinions, was a softer position that accepted any form of the Scriptures, even a paraphrase, that was likely to induce more readers to learn about God and see life from a Judeo-Christian perspective. Formally and publicly, Graham had to adhere to the first standard, or he would have lost his following among conservative religious groups. But practically, he probably realized the absurdity of biblical infallibility and what an impediment it erects between the preacher and modern listeners. So he continued to sound as if he believed in the absolute authority and incontrovertibility of the Scriptures, while really seeking a middle ground where he could relate more easily to people interested in finding God in their lives, not subscribing to some sectarian view of the Bible.

I make no bones about having moved out of the conservative, fundamentalist position on the Scriptures I was taught by the church of my childhood to a far more open, questioning, and adventurous stance. I won't go as far as those who have rejected a majority of the sayings attributed to Jesus in the Gospels, for I think that may be a case of throwing the baby out with the bath water. But I would fight to the death for their right to make such claims and will stand upon at least a portion of their conclusions. We have far less to lose by a free and open approach to the Scriptures than by a mincing, guarded attitude that treats them as too sacrosanct for genuine criticism.

God is never threatened by a critical approach to the Scriptures. Neither is the church. And if God and the church are not threatened by such an approach, then why should the Scriptures themselves be threatened?

Martin Luther wrote a tractate about what he called "the Babylonian captivity of the church" — the imprisonment of the late medieval church in certain practices and prejudices of the Roman ecclesial authority. That title might well be applied to the views of fundamentalists today, who would hold the entire church captive by insisting on their own inflexible attitudes toward the Bible. And just as the Reformation produced new light and energy in the history of the church by rejecting the church's imprisonment, it is important for us to discover new light and energy in our own time by repudiating the biblical views of the fundamentalists.

Although I have never met him, I have long felt a strong kinship to the Episcopal Church's Bishop John Shelby Spong, who served as rector of St. John's Episcopal Church in Lynchburg, Virginia, only a short time prior to my going there as pastor of the First Presbyterian Church. I like very much what Spong says in *Rescuing the Bible from Fundamentalism: A Bishop Rethinks the Meaning of Scripture:* "I come to this study as one who has had a lifetime love affair with this book. I look at the authority of the Scriptures as one who has been both nurtured by and then disillusioned with the literal Bible. My devotion to the Bible was so intense that it led me into a study that finally obliterated any possibility that the Bible could be related to on a literal basis. My relationship to the Bible became and remains so significant that I cannot ignore it, forget it, or walk away from it. I have to engage it, probe it, dissect it, transcend it. It is a volume that has been a source of genuine life for me."[5]

I too have had a lifetime love affair with the Bible. And as I am sure is true for Bishop Spong as well, it is the very fact that I love the Bible so much that drives me to insist on its

true character as a compilation of exploratory words about
God, not the final, irrevocable Word of God as painted by
the fundamentalists. To make of it anything more is to do
it an ultimate disservice. It is in fact to make of the Bible
an idol, and to set it in place of the living God. As Solomon
reminded the people of Israel in his dedicatory prayer for
the new temple, no house can begin to contain the God
in whose honor the temple was erected; and certainly no
book, or collection of books, is able to contain the majesty
and glory of the immeasurable God, the one whose being
lies as far beyond it as my life lies beyond the conceptual
ability of the finches and nuthatches congregating at the
birdfeeder outside my window.

SOMETHING IS HAPPENING at my old home church in Somerset, Kentucky. People are beginning to believe in more than
a literal Bible. As I said, I was back there recently to help
celebrate a big anniversary. I could feel it, could sense it
in the little things people said: they are no longer enslaved
to the idea of inerrant Scriptures. One man, a deacon, even
said, "I like the fresh, imaginative way you deal with a text. It
makes a lot more sense to me than that old Bible-thumpin'
stuff we've heard all our lives!"

The new pastor is still enslaved to a literal approach to the
Scriptures, or pretends to be. He is working on his doctorate
at Southern Baptist Theological Seminary in Louisville, and
would probably be expelled if the officials there got a whiff
of any rebelliousness.

But the people of the church are growing. They are finding the old conservatism inadequate in many ways, especially
when it clashes with their understanding of the world today.
On their television sets, they meet Buddhists and Muslims
and Hindus and Shintoists. More importantly, they meet sec-
ularists and agnostics and technocrats who couldn't care
less about religion. Some of them probably subscribe to

New Age magazine and dabble in aromatherapy and holistic medicine and Eastern meditation. And they are mixing with the Methodists and Disciples and Lutherans and Roman Catholics in the town.

They will be slow to cast off their bondage, for it is hard to do in one's home town. And they will publicly approve the fundamentalist views of their pastor. But inside, where the thaw is occurring, a stream of new thinking is beginning to run, and to erode the magical, superstitious theology of their parents and grandparents that held to a literal Bible and an anthropomorphic notion of God and the sinfulness of homosexuality and a dozen other primitive viewpoints. If I can hasten the thaw even a little by writing this book and sharing some insights from my personal journey, I shall be happy, for that is the commitment I have made. Like the fellow in Plato's "Allegory of the Cave" who stumbled to the mouth of the cave and knew that his friends inside were still fascinated by shadows, I feel compelled to say, "Come and see something better! It may seem radical to you right now, but someday you'll be glad you did."

Second Wrong Teaching

God Is a Great Moral Judge, and Therefore Jesus Had to Die for Our Sins

For God so loved the world, that he gave his only be-gotten Son, that whosoever believeth in him should not perish, but have everlasting life. For God sent not his Son into the world to condemn the world, but that the world through him might be saved.

(John 3:16–17, KJV)

This was my favorite Scripture during my youth, and now I am trying to figure out why. One reason is that it was easy to memorize and quote. Most of the young people in my home church could readily cite it. I said I was proud of my conservative background for the emphasis it put on Scripture. There were lots of verses we could produce from memory. This just happened to be one most of us shared.

Another reason, I believe now, is that it was one of the few biblical passages we knew that actually spoke of God's love. Therefore it presented an antidote to the heavy emphasis in our tradition on God's judgmental side. True, it was the *world* God was said to love, not individuals. But it was easy enough to translate that into something more personal. And in a hard world, it was hopeful to be able to think of God's tenderness toward oneself, even though he continued in the main to be a frightening, magisterial figure.

Conservatives, I have found, live primarily in the Old Testament. They may quote the New Testament as well, but their sympathies are thoroughly with a God of wrath and justice, not one of love and forgiveness.

A friend and former colleague, Dr. James J. H. Price, a professor of religion at Lynchburg College, was once asked by the religion department of the University of Virginia to present a paper on Jerry Falwell's use of the Bible. A diligent student of Falwell's ministry, he did a review of five years' worth of Falwell's sermons, noting both the texts with which he began his sermons and his use of Scripture in the sermons themselves. The result was astonishing: more than 90 percent of Falwell's biblical citations were from the Old Testament.

This raises an interesting question. Are Falwell's pronounced views on militarism, homosexuality, and the judgment of God the result of his preference for the Old Testament, or does he preach so often from the Old Testament because he can find texts there to support his views? Perhaps if he were a more avid student of the New Testament — the synoptic Gospels in particular — his entire persona as a preacher would be different.

When I was growing up, we heard about Jesus in every service of worship. But no distinction was ever offered between his understanding of God and the understanding of God in the Old Testament. Because the Bible was regarded as a monolithic book, all literally inspired, it never occurred to our ministers and teachers that biblical concepts might change between the time of Abraham and Moses in the Old Testament and Jesus and the disciples in the New. So the Jesus we got was a Jesus who believed in the God of ancient Judaism — the one who laid down all those harsh punishments in Deuteronomy and Leviticus and often encouraged the Jews to destroy even the wives and children of their enemies.

Our pastor sometimes preached from the Gospels, especially on Palm Sunday (though we never celebrated it as part of a formal church year) and Easter. But his favorite parts of the New Testament were clearly the writings of Paul and the letter to the Hebrews, which he assumed was also by Paul, as the King James Version of the Scriptures said it was. He seemed particularly wed to the Book of Romans and the Book of Hebrews, because he delighted in talking about the Jewish sacrificial system and how Christianity was an extension of it. So I grew up with heavy doses of what I later learned to call "penal theology," or theology emphasizing God's inviolable sense of justice and the death of Jesus as satisfaction of the legal payment for our sins. We loved to sing such hymns as "The Old Rugged Cross," "Alas, And Did My Savior Bleed?," "Jesus Paid It All," "Nailed to the Cross," and "When I Survey the Wondrous Cross," all passionate testimonies to our faith in the one whose life had been sacrificially exchanged for ours.

Now LET ME RUSH TO AGREE that there is a strain of penal theology in the New Testament. St. Paul undoubtedly found it one of his best lines of argument when trying to persuade the Jews, who were his primary target for the Gospel, that Christianity was no new religion, but the actual fulfillment of the religion of their fathers and forefathers. The Book of Hebrews is built on penal theology almost entirely, again emphasizing to Jews that Jesus was both high priest and sacrifice, performing once and for all the action of Israel's priests by giving his own life as the perfect sacrifice, so that no further sacrifice would ever be needed.

I understand all of that, and I know that the theology of atonement appeals to people who carry around a strong sense of personal guilt. In fact, the sermon that originally brought me to Christ played exactly this theme. The visiting evangelist told a story in our Sunday school assembly about a poor, hungry boy in a country school who secretly ate another child's lunch sandwich. The teacher demanded to know who had taken the sandwich. When the boy admitted that he had, the teacher said he must come to the desk and receive a caning. The sight of his thin little body when he removed his shirt struck remorse into every heart in the room, but the teacher was resolute — justice must be served. Suddenly a big, strapping lad in the back of the classroom asked, "Teacher, is there anything in the rules that says someone else can't take his whipping for him?" When the teacher said no, the boy came forward, removing his shirt. He bent across the desk and took the other boy's caning.

"And that, boys and girls," said the evangelist, "is what Jesus did for you. The Bible says, 'He was wounded for our transgressions, he was bruised for our iniquities: the chastisement of our peace was upon him; and with his stripes we are healed.'"

This image of substitutionary atonement spoke eloquently to my tender heart. I was just entering preadolescence, and I am sure there was much I felt guilty about. I was beginning to have confusing thoughts about sex and my attraction to females. I had been brought up in a puritanical environment and knew I had failed my family and society in many ways. God was such a total mystery to me that I had not tried very hard to think about him, and I knew I must be considered a complete outsider to him. My parents did not get along, and I am certain I felt at least partly responsible for that. There was practically nothing of which I could boast, nothing that would offset this tremendous deficit in my personal accounts. Telling me that Jesus had died in my place, had received the stripes intended for me, had a very powerful effect on me. Of course I wanted a savior who bore all my sin!

As a pastor, I have often counseled with people who had a deep, almost ineffaceable sense of guilt because they too were reared in a culture of guilt and shame. I remember one woman in New Jersey who was so supersensitive to her sins that often she was unable to receive Communion in church, and would sit trembling and agitated as it was being served. She was a very intelligent woman, and we had long discussions about this problem. I found it ironic that she insisted on coming to Communion with a feeling of righteousness, for as I argued with her, the words of Communion speak of the cup as "my blood, which is shed for you." She could not get beyond Paul's admonition, however, about examining oneself before receiving Communion, for eating and drinking unworthily is tantamount to eating and drinking damnation. I tried to persuade her that Paul was talking about something else, a situation in which people were behaving frivolously about the Lord's Supper, but my words were of no avail. She was so convinced of God's moral judgment in her life, even as she contemplated taking Communion, that she could not receive the grace that might easily have changed her situation.

I am not arguing that human beings bring no guilt to the encounter with God and therefore require no atonement. Certainly there are great moral outrages that beg some mighty act of forgiveness before they can even begin to be obliterated and healed. My wife and I recently spent an afternoon in the United States Holocaust Memorial in Washington, D.C., and came away under a cloud of sadness that would not go away for several days. The enormity of the crimes of Hitler and the Nazis against humanity — the brutal manner in which they interrupted the lives of millions of people, punishing and torturing and killing them for practically no reason at all — demonstrates some great skewedness at the heart of the human situation.

I remember once having a dream after reading Dostoevsky's *Crime and Punishment*. Like Rashkolnikov, I had murdered an old woman for her money and was desperately seeking to avoid discovery. I woke soaked with perspiration. The realization that I could even dream of such a terrible deed haunted me for days, and I have been wary ever since of saying I could not possibly be capable of an inhuman act.

But this is still no argument for a God who must be placated by human sacrifice. And to assume, as many conservatives do, that Calvin was right and that even infants are besmirched by sin and must be covered by the blood of Christ for salvation is a terrible thing. It is one thing to speak assuredly of human depravity, as Paul does when he says that if we say we have no sin, we deceive ourselves. But it is quite another thing to use those words of his, as conservatives do, to paint human nature in the very worst of terms, as though we were all inwardly cankered and worthless.

Maybe the problem with most conservatives is that they have no sense of humor. They live with the bleakest, most grudging estimates of human value. Fortunately most people do not pay much attention to them anymore and give them wide berth as mere doomsayers and false prophets. But it is sad for those who do still take them seriously and seek to shape their spiritual lives by the lasts these stingy cobblers have cut.

WHAT IS GOD REALLY LIKE? We may be surprised when we learn. As the punch line of the old joke has it, "She's black."

There is one rule I think we're safe in evoking: that God is better and more than we can imagine. So if we can imagine God as a tender, loving parent, God must be that and more. If we think of God as an aura, a spiritual being inducing ecstasy in the soul entrusted to him, God is surely that and more as well.

Did God require Jesus to die for the atonement of the world? No, certainly not in any literal sense. What God required of Jesus is what God has always required of his people, that they be faithful. "What does the Lord require of you,

O man, but to do justly, to love mercy, and to walk humbly with your God?" (Micah 6:8). Jesus knew this. It is why he endured the agony he did in the garden of Gethsemane. Facing a violent death — a shameful death, even — was the test of his faithfulness to God. God did not say to Jesus in the garden, "Now, son, I want you to go out there and get killed tomorrow for the sins of the world." Some of Jesus' enthusiastic followers might later add that spin to the meaning of his death. But Jesus really died the way many of his followers have died, standing up for what they believed in the face of overwhelming odds and refusing to compromise their integrity in order to get off with their lives — or their jobs or their dignity.

Did Jesus know he was going to die? Very likely. At least he knew the price he might pay by going to Jerusalem when the political climate there was so hotly charged against him. Did he believe he was going to die for the sins of the world? Highly unlikely. His statements about this are almost entirely in the Fourth Gospel, the most fictional and contrived of all the Gospels. The author of this Gospel did not write the life of Jesus; he rewrote it. He took the salient materials of the other Gospels and added a special twist to create a sublime narrative about a God who became man in order that men might become God — or at least live with God.

As Robert W. Funk puts it in *Honest to Jesus,* "In the Fourth Gospel the pretense of a flesh-and-blood figure is dropped: Jesus has been made coeternal with the Father and he doesn't mind telling us so in episode after episode. The history of Jesus the man has been smothered by the myth of the Christ."[6]

Does this mean the Fourth Gospel is untrue? No. Fiction is often truer than life. But does it mean that we are bound to the fictionalism of this Gospel for the facts of our theology? By no means. It is like the songs we sing in church. They may do more to set our thinking about spiritual matters than they ought, but they are merely songs, doxologies, poetic rhapsodies of faith, not to be taken literally except by the extremely literal-minded.

To some extent, the same is true of all the Gospels, and certainly of the rest of the Bible. We read them and hear them read to us. They help to form the environment of our souls, to create an atmosphere in which we live and move and have our beings. But only the conservative mind restricts them to being truthful and factual, and fails to regard them as music by which to dance and revel and live one's life.

The nature of God is the great mystery of the universe, the secret sought by all mystics and contemplatives, whether Jewish, Christian, Hindu, or whatever. The trick of discovering the mystery is to learn how to see the clues that abound in our universe, that literally overwhelm the mind and heart once one has become accustomed to spotting them. This is the message of Edna St. Vincent Millay's poem "God's World," with its lines,

> Long have I known a glory in it all,
> But never knew like this;
> Here such a pattern is
> As stretcheth me apart. Lord, I do fear
> Thou'st made the world too beautiful this year.
> My soul is all but out of me — let fall
> No burning leaf; prithee, let no bird call.[7]

For my own part, there are days when God appears as close to me as the patch of violets I stumble upon beside a woodland path, as the cardinal and the chickadee eating together at the feeder outside our dinette window, even as the lowly bagworm suspended from the tip of a fir tree beside our porch. When my wife and I stroll under the ethereal cherry blossoms around the reflecting basin at the Jefferson Memorial in Washington, D.C., I am struck speechless. Sometimes it happens as I sit in a restaurant watching an old couple at another table. He is having difficulty with a trembling hand raising a fork to bring food to his mouth. She watches patiently, and only occasionally reaches out to steady the hand, always with such love and devotion in her eyes. It can occur as I sit in my study beholding a magnificent sunset across the Blue Ridge Mountains, or smell the cleansing, pungent aroma of a freshly cut lemon, or stare at the miracle of words on my computer screen.

The world really is the body of God, signaling the presence of a mind and spirit that sets bushes to burning before awestruck Moseses around the globe, at every second of every day.

I never heard anything about this God in the church I attended. The God I heard about there was a pain in the ass, if you'll pardon the expression. He was jealous, imperious, demanding, inflicting, peevish, and resentful. He was powerful, but he was also mean and vengeful, and never really overlooked or forgot one's sins. Even if he was said to forgive them through the blood of Jesus, there was always the implication that they were written down in a great book somewhere and would be brought out at the most embarrassing moment, like some family skeleton trundled out by a malicious uncle just when the bishop had come to call.

Like Walter Harrelson's Aunt Zora, I knew there was something wrong about this God, though I was too young and inexperienced to put my finger on what it was. Even my childish mind aspired to something nobler and more forgiving than a God of righteousness whose offended dignity always required appeasing, even after he professed to have forgotten the offense.

It was only after I had got beyond the idea of a literal Bible that I was free to experience God as more than anything I could imagine — as the great creative spirit still at work in an exploding universe, still shaping beauty and love and meaning at the heart of everything. The other God had robbed me of the world, for he was always demanding fealty and attention, jealous if I thought of anything else. This God, on the other hand, rewarded me with his affection and self-disclosures in proportion as I turned away from him and looked in other directions, where I was always discovering that everything was a part of him, everything whispered his name, everything sang his praises.

Now I understand "law" and "righteousness" differently, because I have found this other God. Before, those concepts were factual, negative things — prison walls with shredded glass and razor wire on the parapets. I was always being cut by them, turned back upon my failure, rebuffed in my desire to live. But when the new God revealed himself, I realized that his law — the part uncontaminated by embellishing scribes — was merely a kind of grace, a mapping of life's mine-field so we wouldn't step disastrously and destroy ourselves. And the righteousness was only awesomeness, a holiness of love and beauty and grace at the heart of divine existence. It was the breath, the intimate warmth, of the More-Than-I-Could-Ever-Imagine, and it was gift, as the warming from the sun is a gift, or the cooling from a spring found deep in the great woods.

Is GOD ALL-POWERFUL, as my pastor and Sunday-school teachers always said he is? They had a special thing about the word *omnipotent*. The ring of the Latin syllables was particularly comforting to them, especially during the dark days of World War II, when gold stars hung in the front windows of those who had lost sons and we were all living from day to day out of ration-coupon books. God was omnipotent, and we would soon be victorious in this great war. We sang "The Battle Hymn of the Republic" a lot, and enjoyed picturing the deity loosing "the fateful lightning of His terrible swift sword" against the Germans and the Japanese.

In 1971, there was great fanfare when Dr. Herschel H.

Hobbs's revised edition of *The Baptist Faith and Message* was released by Convention Press in Nashville. Hobbs was one of the best-known and most widely respected figures among Southern Baptists. Longtime minister of the First Baptist Church of Oklahoma City and once president of the Southern Baptist Convention, he had spoken in most of the large churches of the denomination. Millions of people trusted his version of this venerable document as if it were the last word on Christian theology. *The Baptist Faith and Message* listed the "Attributes of God," and under that heading, the characteristic of "Omnipotence": "God possesses all power. He can do anything in keeping with his nature and purpose. The only limits to his power are self-imposed. He cannot lie or act contrary to his own laws, character, and purposes. These limitations are evidences of God's power, not of his weakness."[8]

One of my preaching mentors, Dr. Paul E. Scherer, was for many years minister of Holy Trinity Lutheran Church and professor of preaching at Union Theological Seminary in New York. Later, when he retired to Princeton as visiting professor of preaching, it was my privilege to serve as his teaching assistant. His mother was a Killinger and had come from the area in Pennsylvania where my grandfather was born, so we always called one another "cousin." My distinguished cousin had a marvelous sermon outline, which I think he liked best of the thousands he had invented in a lifetime of preaching. It had three points, as many sermons did in those days:

1. What if God were power without love?

2. What if God were love without power?

3. What if God were power in love with us?

It is a very fetching outline, I think, and I imagine it has been preached from thousands of pulpits, because Dr. Scherer was always free to share it with other ministers.

But what about the God of power? Where was the power in the Inquisition, when people were tortured for not confessing the right kind of faith? Or the Holocaust, when all those hapless Jews were boxed off to work sites and death camps, their possessions confiscated, even the gold fillings knocked out of their teeth and their hair cropped off to stuff mattresses and living-room furniture? Or, for that matter, when Jesus was crucified on a barren knoll outside Jerusalem?

What is power anyway? What does it mean in a deity? Isn't it simply an analogue derived from the image of an ancient potentate, a king or an emperor who exercised total control over the slaves and sycophants in his territory? Jesus apparently rejected such a definition of power. We assume he could have provoked a revolution of such power had he chosen to do so, for he once slipped away when people wanted to make him a king and bade Simon Peter to put away his sword in Gethsemane. But apparently he saw beyond the emptiness of such control over people's lives and knew that the real kingdom of God is not and never had been established on a basis of sheer force or power.

Jesus explored another kind of power — moral and spiritual power, power not of this world, power that often appears powerless in the economic or political arena, power to choose love and integrity and faithfulness over earthly gain. For two millennia now, artists have been trying to unpack the potency of Jesus' gesture, the deathless value of his choice to die a free man in a shackled society. What he did endures precisely because it is the kind of power available to all of us, whether we live in Kosovo or Pakistan or Zimbabwe or South Carolina. It alone is "the power of God unto salvation."

It is the power Sir Thomas More imitated in Robert Bolt's play *A Man for All Seasons*. Refusing to condone his sovereign Henry VIII's divorce, More paid for it with his life. As he stepped up to the executioner's block, he comforted the bladesman about to despatch his soul: "Friend, be not afraid of your office. You send me to God."[9] The practitioner of this power wields a moral superiority in a world where brute force is never the final word, where God and a heavenly kingdom are always waiting as reward and solace.

Is God omnipotent? No, not in the literal sense of that word. As some wag rightly asked, "Can God make a rock too heavy for him to lift?" The Calvinists are great casuists and have developed long arguments to provide for divine fore-knowledge and to distinguish between that and free will, so that God can appear all-powerful, yet have his bets hedged in dealing with human beings. It is all really quite ridiculous. We don't have to protect God's honor and glory. If he has even a modicum of the power attributed to him, he can well take care of himself.

We had better hope God is *not* really omnipotent, for if he is, then he immediately becomes liable for all the tragedies that occur in his world — the floods that destroy thousands in Afghanistan, the plagues that carry off tens of thousands in rural Africa, the tornadoes that rip through homes where children are sleeping and churches where people are wor-shiping. He might also be responsible for the devastating wars of the twentieth century, and the flu epidemics and the global economic crash and AIDS and a few other things on our list of grievances.

The God I love is a *limited* God — limited as all artists are limited, as all builders are limited, as all parents are lim-ited. The very nature of action is that it involves limitation. Whatever is done or said establishes constructs that would be violated if something else were done or said. The God still creating the world — we will come back to that idea in a moment — is unavoidably hampered by the very things he does, finds his power restricted by what he has already es-tablished. If he makes gooseberries, they cannot taste like blackberries. If he allows the unleashing of the atom, he cannot deter scientists who want to make bombs.

Maybe when I was a young man in a conservative church I thought I had to have a God of unlimited power, but not anymore. I probably thought my father was all-powerful when I was a small boy and he was a towering giant of a man who could lift great weights and raise a garden and drive a car across the United States. But years later, when my father was old and feeble and I became his principal caretaker, it did not matter to me that I was wrong about his power; what I wanted from him then was love and relationship, not protection or physical assistance or financial aid. What I want from God now is fellowship, the kind of spiritual unity with him that Jesus promised his disciples at the Last Supper. One of my teachers, Paul Tillich, loved to call God "the Ground of all being," and what I want now is to be intimately related to that Ground, to be at home in God, to know, in a world of whirling concepts and allegiances, that I am bonded with the most creative One I have ever known.

God cannot or will not violate physical laws to improve my physical health, my financial condition, or anything else about me. I am adult enough not to expect that. But God and I together are in one sense indomitable. No other power in all the world is able to overcome our union, to drive us apart. This is what Paul was feeling when he wrote his great peroration in Romans 8: "Who will separate us from the love of Christ? Will hardship, or distress, or persecution, or famine, or nakedness, or peril, or sword? ... No, in all these things we are more than conquerors through him who loved us. For I am convinced that neither death, nor life, nor angels, nor rulers, nor things present, nor things to come, nor powers, nor height, nor depth, nor anything else in all creation, will be able to separate us from the love of God in Christ Jesus our Lord" (Romans 8:35–39).

A spiritually mature person doesn't insist on flawless days, perfect health, or mastery over the world. No, he or she wants only union with the Beloved, and knows that union is there, already existing, whatever earthly powers may try to corrupt or destroy it. God doesn't need to be omnipotent. God only needs to be the Ground of all being, the Center of our fellowship, the Basis of spiritual love and unity.

I SAID WE WOULD COME BACK to the notion that God is still creating the world, that he has never really finished what he began billions of years ago. Conservatives and fundamentalists don't like such talk, of course, for in their literally inspired, inerrant Bible everything is neatly sealed up in the first few chapters of the Book of Genesis. Faculty members in Southern Baptist theological seminaries, in fact, are required to sign an "Abstract of Principles," saying they believe the world was actually created in only six days and that all the other "miracles" in the Bible are literally true. I am always amazed that even one seminary can find enough knowledgeable teachers to perjure themselves this way, let alone half a dozen.

But anybody who knows anything about geology and biology realizes that nothing on our planet, indeed, nothing in the entire universe, remains the same. Everything is wheeling and gyring and constantly undergoing change. God is probably only in the early stages of creating the world and humanity. Now that he has revealed the secrets of the computer to us, we shall behold transformations at an exponential rate. Technologists say that the human mind itself will be vastly altered in the next hundred years by the fact that increasing numbers of us sit at keyboards surfing the Internet, sending and receiving e-mail, and doing our work with the aid of sophisticated programs most of us don't understand. Change, evolution, transformation comes to everything — except possibly the conservative mind.

Who or what is God? Certainly there are elements of the Judeo-Christian deity in him — creator, caller, sustainer, leader, redeemer, wooer, shepherd, lover, inspirer. In the

case of a war like the one waged by the Allies against the demonic Central Forces in World War II, he may conceivably
have a little of the warrior-god about him. But he is so much
more than our traditional conceptualism begins to describe.
Alfred North Whitehead once called him "a tender care that
nothing be lost."[10] I often think of that at a funeral. He is
preserver, includer, the indefatigable host who never rests in
his intention of bringing everybody to the table, especially
those who have been marginalized, penalized, or brutalized
in any way.

God is the highly Benevolent Mind and Intelligent Heart
behind every good and noble spiritual impulse we ever
have, the Great Magnet arranging molecules into ultimately
meaningful patterns, the Kindly Light shedding luminescence on every shadowy conundrum and into every dark
and puzzling corner, the Parenting Force guiding wayward
children home, the Restless Spirit urging us ever onward
toward love and fulfillment. He's also the Comforting One
who is always there to take over when we have reached the
end of our strength or have sent everything around us into a
tailspin, the Generous Giver whose life and love and energy
flow moment by moment into our tiny receptacles and keep
us moving on toward a city not made with hands, and a deity
who only begins to be defined by anthropomorphisms.

Does this God require the death of Jesus or anybody else
in order to make up with sinners and throw his arms around
them? We shouldn't insult him that way. Substitutionary
atonement was a workable image among people who understood the offering of sacrifices for everything from good
health to plump yearlings to a bumper crop. But we can do
a lot better than that, and should, in a world that has passed
through several new cultural periods since then.

We never completely give up our atavistic notions of the
deity, particularly those ingrained in our earliest years. I still
pray for my children and my friends who have cancer and

offer thanks for bright days and good food, despite a mental recognition that life is pretty much a wheel of fortune, and there are plenty of people in the world far better than I who nevertheless get visited with the most unspeakable tragedies and afflictions. And I have a strong sense of well-being in God as my Father, the New Testament image that has always spoken most deeply to me. But I chide myself from time to time about being spiritually lazy, about not participating more imaginatively in the exploration of God's fuller being in a day of space travel and computer technology. Being comfortable with old understandings of God is no excuse for not living at the edge of our abilities. We *can* discover new images and formulas for his role in a universe expanding both externally and internally at fantastic rates, and we can risk throwing ourselves more completely than ever into the union with him that is capable of redeeming everything.

Third Wrong Teaching

Jesus Is the Only Way to God

In 1980, Southern Baptists made the headlines at a gathering of religious politicians in Dallas when their president, a pastor named Bailey Smith, announced that "God Almighty does not hear the prayer of a Jew. For how in the world can God hear the prayer of a man who says that Jesus Christ is not the true Messiah?" People around the nation reacted as if such a sentiment were news. I grew up with it. The pastors and teachers of my conservative church knew all along that God doesn't listen to Jews any more than he listens to Buddhists, Muslims, or Hindus. They also knew he doesn't listen to Catholics and Mormons. They even hedged a little on Methodists, Disciples, and Presbyterians, not being completely sure about them.

Baptists and other dyed-in-the-wool conservatives have this thing about Jesus, that since the incarnation two thousand years ago he is absolutely the only way to God for anything, whether we're talking prayer or salvation. So Jesus, who in person was the great leveler, the wonderful unifier always breaking down walls and reaching out to the unredeemed and untouchable, has ironically become the great divider, separating people into the saved and the unsaved, the righteous and the unrighteous. Today, more than anything else, he prevents his followers' acceptance of Muslims, Jews, Hindus, Buddhists, Shintoists, pantheists, and liberals.

The main proof-text of this position is John 14:6, where Jesus says, "I am the way, and the truth, and the life. No one comes to the Father except through me." That sounds unequivocal enough, and would be, if we could accept the literalist point of view that everything in the Bible means exactly what it says and carries the divine imprimatur on it. But it overlooks completely the semi-fictional character of the Gospel of John and the rhetorical situation in which Jesus speaks these words. Actually, the saying is one of the famous "I am" sayings of Jesus in the Gospel — e.g., "I am the bread of life," "I am the good shepherd," "I am the true vine" — all of which serve to establish a Christology considerably higher and more supernatural than that of the other three Gospels.

John's Gospel begins on an exceptionally high note, proclaiming Jesus as the Word of God who existed with God from the very beginning and helped to create the world, and proceeds with the story of a savior always a little more divine than human to a dramatic series of Resurrection accounts at its end. The Jesus of this Gospel always appears more self-aware than the Jesus of the other Gospels, if not transcendently arrogant. Unlike the Jesus of the other Gospels, he doesn't bother to teach in parables and collections of sayings. Instead, he regards it as enough that he speaks to people at all, and almost everything he says and does is heavily freighted with symbolism. For example, his ministry opens with the story of the wedding at Cana, where he changes water to wine, connoting the improvement of his spiritual gift over that of Judaism, for the water stood in six vats (a number suggesting incompleteness) and was used for ceremonial cleansing under traditional Jewish law (John 2:1–11). Then Jesus cleanses the temple in Jerusalem, denouncing the money changers and sellers of sheep, cattle, and doves for making his Father's house a marketplace (John 2:12–22).

Why has John moved this story of the temple from the end of Jesus' life, where it was placed by the other Gospel narrators? Because it seemed to him a fitting public act, after the story of the water and wine, for commencing the ministry. It served notice on the spiritually crass and greedy merchants who occupied the holy city that something higher and better was about to displace them!

The point is, this favorite saying of the conservatives about Jesus' being the only way to God the Father occurs in a completely histrionic and somewhat unreliable Gospel — unreliable from a factual standpoint — where it is obviously the product of an evolution in Christian teaching from the simpler, more unretouched portraits of the earlier Gospels to the iconographic picture of this one.

THE SECOND-CHOICE PROOF-TEXT of the conservatives is Acts 4:12, in which Simon Peter is speaking to the Jewish council after he and the Apostle John have been arrested for proclaiming the resurrection of the dead. When the council asks Peter the source of authority for what he and John are preaching, he says they speak in the name of Jesus Christ of Nazareth, "whom you crucified, whom God raised from the dead." Then he says, "There is salvation in no one else, for there is no other name under heaven given among mortals by which we must be saved."

It is the polemical answer we should expect under the circumstances. The raison d'être given for Christianity in the Book of Acts, our at-times-somewhat-dubious "history" of the early church, is that it is the Spirit-filled extension of Israel's own mission — to be the salvation of the world. As Israel failed or renegged on its promises to God, God raised up Jesus as the unlikely messiah leading a new Israel, consisting of the followers converted to his leadership. Naturally, Peter, as spokesman for the early Christian cause, would answer the leaders of the old Judaism thus: salvation has come down to Jesus, and there is nowhere else we should be looking for it.

But again it is highly curious that Jesus himself, in the earlier Gospels of the Christian way, never defined himself in such exclusivist terms. For my own part, I keep coming back to the parable he told about the Pharisee and the tax collector, in which the Pharisee stood in the temple and thanked God that he was better than other people, especially the tax collector he recognized there. The tax collector, obviously humbled even to appear in the temple, was overtaken by remorse, and prayed, "God, be merciful to me, a sinner!" "I tell you," said Jesus, "this man went down to his home justified rather than the other; for all who exalt themselves will be humbled, but all who humble themselves will be exalted" (Luke 18:14).

Note that this story is told in the Gospel of Luke, the same Luke who authored the Book of Acts, containing the saying, "There is salvation in no one else, for there is no other name under heaven given among mortals by which we must be saved." Yet Jesus, having told the story of the Pharisee and the tax collector, does not instruct his disciples, "Now go quickly and tell this man about what God is doing in me, and he will be saved!" Jesus says simply that he "went down to his home justified" — the word means "made righteous," and is a key word in the soteriology of both the Old and the New Testaments. The man *did not have to know the name of Jesus.* He was a humble man before God, aware of his shortcomings, asking for divine mercy. He fulfilled the fundamental test of redemption stated in Micah 6:8, "He has told you, O mortal, what is good; and what does the Lord require of you but to do justice, and to love kindness, and to walk humbly with your God?" It would have been redundant for Jesus to have insisted on some formulaic recognition of himself from the man. That was not Jesus' character, or the role he was intended to play.

OF COURSE CHRISTIANS find something special in Christ. They ought to. Were it not for him, they would not have been grafted into Israel's stock, to use Paul's metaphor from the Book of Romans. Heaven knows where they — we — would have wound up in the panorama of world beliefs and religious understandings, had we not encountered the gospel of Christ.

But it has always seemed somehow ironic, and not a little offensive, that we should use Jesus, who taught universal love and acceptance, as a means of furthering discord and disalliance. It is unworthy of him, and an unnatural part of the religion that has grown up around his name. We glorify him today precisely because he was self-effacing, because he accepted death on a cross and the ignominy that went with it, instead of starting a protest-war against the religious authorities of Judaism. To turn him around and make him less than self-effacing, to insist on the contrary that he is the only way by which people can come to the Father about whom he taught, is to subvert his own beliefs and purposes.

I have long had a fond admiration for E. Stanley Jones, the great Methodist missionary widely known for his eagerness to hold dialogues with the religious leaders of India. In his famous Ashrams, or Round Table discussions, Jones invited leaders of several faiths to sit down together and talk openly of their spiritual experience and religious beliefs. It was a dangerous thing for all of them, he said, for each, including himself, risked being changed by what he heard. Yet for him it was the only way to approach the matter of witness in our time. As he said in his book *Christ at the Round Table,* "The Crusaders conquered Jerusalem and found in the end that Christ was not there. They had lost Him through the very spirit and methods by which they sought to serve Him."[11] It is true, he admitted, that the passion of evangelism suffers from a loss of mindless superiority; but Christ profits from a humbler, more reasonable approach.

One of the things Jones found in his work in India was that most Buddhists, Hindus, Bhaktis, and others had a profound respect for Jesus — even Gandhi admitted that he learned a great deal from him — and that the most inhibiting factor in that respect was the religion that had grown up around Jesus, or the church and its practitioners. "Christlikeness" and "un-Christlikeness," he discovered, were not only acceptable tests for behavior among Indian philosophers, but the favored tests. In other words, Jesus was making his way among Indians, if Christians would just not muck up his progress by being so imperial and demanding of them.

The one thing Jones found lacking in most Indians of whatever religion — and they usually admitted this — was the great joy often seen in Christians. The Indians professed not to have had any kind of conversion experience; they had grown gradually and thoughtfully into the views that now characterized their religious perspectives. Christians, on the other hand, often claim to have been found by Christ in some moment of need or perplexity and, in companionship with him, to have entered a new plane of existence where following him is exhilarating.

In the end, after long and patient discussions with many Indians, Jones pled the superiority of his own faith: "Jesus is Religion. He is not a religion, or the religion, but Religion itself. I cannot be satisfied with a mathematics, but only with Mathematics, the truth about the mathematical world. I do not want an astronomy, but Astronomy, the truth about the stars. I crave not an ethics, but Ethics, the truth about the moral universe. So I cannot be satisfied with a religion, or even with the religion, but only with Religion, the truth about our moral and spiritual universe. I can only be satisfied with Jesus, who is Religion."[12]

This is what I mean when I say that Christians should find something special in Christ. If we didn't, we would probably all become Buddhists or Muslims or something else — eclecticists, at least, forging our own belief-systems out of bits and pieces of the many religions and philosophies we have encountered. But holding Christ in great reverence, and attributing to him the honor of saying he is the very incarnation of God and our appointed leader, is very different from insisting that no one can come to the Father except through him. This attitude bespeaks an unforgivable arrogance and an incredible lack of compassion.

Bruce Bawer puts his finger on it in his book *Stealing Jesus,* in which he says that contemporary conservatism and fundamentalism in religion is essentially a revival of ancient legalism, in which a particular kind of Christian today brands everyone who is not of his her rigid way of regarding Christ as lost and inferior. It is actually a new Phariseeism, precisely the sort of self-preening religious attitude that Jesus attacked in his time as being subspiritual, noncompassionate, and blind to the true nature and will of God.[13]

MY WIFE AND I were attending a Baptist church in Birmingham, Alabama — one of the few Baptist churches in that fundamentalist city where we could sometimes feel a genuine spirit of worship. The pastor happened to be away that Sunday, and there was a visiting missionary. During the first fifteen minutes of the liturgy, the missionary's wife appeared on the pulpit dais wearing the chador of a Muslim woman. She was going to present the children's sermon for the morning, and so had a large group of children gathered about her. She gave herself a Muslim name and pretended to be a woman of the African culture where she and her husband worked. We were pleased and intrigued — until suddenly she whipped off the outfit and began a diatribe against Muslims, saying they were all lost in sin and had no hope of salvation without Jesus. She even quoted the passage from the Fourth Gospel about Jesus' being the only way to the Father.

Later, my wife narrated this experience to a friend of ours

who had once been a missionary to another African country. It was obvious, as she got into the story, that our friend saw nothing wrong with the woman's approach. I could tell my wife felt as if she had Evel Knieveled herself out into midair with the story and was going to have difficulty landing without hurting our friend's feelings.

"But don't you believe that Jesus is the only way to salvation?" asked our friend. "How can you be a Christian if you don't believe that?"

It is very hard to convince conservative Christians that there are good Muslims and good Hindus and good Buddhists and good Jews and good Universalists who enjoy a close relationship with God and, if the Christian idea of heaven is accurate, may well be in heaven along with them. Some Christians, I believe, are more prepared to see dogs and cats in heaven — especially their own beloved animals — than human beings who have not verbally confessed to being followers of Jesus Christ.

Bawer says they are lacking in compassion. Perhaps so, but I do not think that was the case with the friend I mentioned above. She is a woman of tender feelings who genuinely cares about other people and their sufferings. I believe it is a matter of training and indoctrination. People raised in most conservative churches have had the idea of Christian exclusivism dinned into them from the time they were small children. We took our child out of a Baptist Sunday school — he was only three at the time — when he came out of his class bearing a tract entitled "Teaching Your Three-Year-Old What Baptists Believe." One of the areas of recommended indoctrination included the idea that there is no redemption outside of Jesus.

I admit that my own training along these lines was hard to surmount. Two of my closest friends in high school were twin Jewish boys. Their parents were Russian Orthodox Jews, who took their children to a synagogue eighty miles from where we lived. I cared about them and worried about their souls' salvation. I wanted to talk about Jesus to them, to witness to them in the traditional fashion. But something stopped me. They were extremely fine young men, and their parents were among the kindest, most considerate people in our community. For years I prayed for their salvation, but I never once broached the subject of Christianity with them. I'm glad now I didn't. We have remained friends through the years, and I continue to see them periodically. I no longer worry about their salvation. I know that, like the tax collector in Jesus' parable, they are justified.

It worried me a great deal when I was a young Christian that my father was not a confessed believer. I tried on two or three occasions to talk with him about it, but he wouldn't tolerate such conversations. I know that he grew up under a strong, dominant father, who was an elder in the Methodist church in a small town in Iowa. In the first community we lived in after I was born, my parents occasionally went to church together — very rarely — either with the Methodists or with the Baptists. I can remember hearing men tease my father about not having seen him in church for a long time. I don't know if it was that or something worse that set him against the church, but he stopped going and would have nothing to do with Christianity. He was very disappointed when I announced I was going to become a minister and told me not to expect any help from him.

Given my indoctrination as a young Christian, I was persuaded that my father would go to hell when he died because he did not confess Christ or go to church. When I found it impossible to talk with him on the subject, I once resorted to a detestable method of attempting to reach him: I enclosed some religious tracts in the birthday present I sent him from college.

I have always been heartily ashamed of that. How presumptuous it was, and how invasive of his privacy! I can imagine how repulsed he must have been when he opened a gift and discovered lying within the wrappings a fundamentalist brochure entitled "What Must I Do to Be Saved?" Perhaps he hurled the gift and the tract — box, wrappings, and all — across the room. How dreadfully that mean-spirited, self-righteous little tract polluted the loving intention of a present!

But my understanding of Christ and his relationship with non-Christians was so muddled at that time. Recalling it, I can easily empathize with our missionary friend, and even with the missionary who condemned all Muslims as lying outside God's pale of acceptance and redemption. It was the way we were trained in a conservative church.

The person who most helped me transcend my youthful indoctrination was a Jew named Harry May. Harry was a rabbi with a Ph.D. from the University of Prague in Czechoslovakia. He came to the U.S. in 1938, when the Nazi purge began, and eventually worked as a chaplain at a university in California. Then he came to Vanderbilt Divinity School while I was teaching there to replace the professor of Jewish studies on sabbatical leave for a year, and he remained in Nashville as a professor of history at the University of Tennessee.

A large, boisterous man with an infectious laugh and incredible knowledge of history, philosophy, and languages, Harry for some reason settled on me as his best friend at Vanderbilt. He invited my family and me to visit him and his family for a Sunday afternoon and evening. We went swimming in their pool, and Harry fixed blintzes for us — the first we had ever had — and served them with Mogen David wine.

When Harry and his wife came to our house, my wife set a big platter of ham on the table, not even thinking about our guests' being Jewish. Harry laughed and brushed it aside. "I'll say a little prayer and make it kosher," he said.

He mumbled a few nonsense syllables over the ham, then announced, "Now it's turkey!"

Later, when Harry and his wife divorced and he remarried, this time to a young Protestant girl who had been one of his students, we often celebrated Jewish holidays with them, and they visited frequently in our home.

Harry and I often talked about our respective faiths and how much they meant to us. He wrote a book about Maimonides, the medieval Jewish mystic, and asked me to read the manuscript. In turn he sometimes read my sermons and commented on them, remarking on the parts that he found helpful or inspiring. I loved the man. We never met anywhere — in our homes, on the street, at the university — without exchanging a crushing hug. We continued to write one another for years, always long, personal letters. A year or so before Harry died, we arranged a meeting back in Nashville — he was living in Michigan and I in Alabama — and had several hours in a restaurant reminiscing about our history together and catching up on what was happening in our lives.

If any man I ever knew was close to God, Harry was. He could be a rogue at times, but he was never a blasphemer. God was too special to him for that. We were brothers in the divine kingdom. I have no doubt of that. I did not have to evangelize Harry. That would have been ludicrous. Here was a man of vast learning and simple faith who recited the Psalms in Hebrew and inventoried his life for repentance every Yom Kippur and lived life as if God were present in the very room where he was enjoying it.

Harry understood about Jesus and my relationship with him. He once said, "If it weren't for Jesus, we wouldn't have become friends." That was true. As I said, Jesus is the reason we were grafted onto the stock of Israel. Harry himself regarded Jesus as a prophet, a teacher of righteousness, and a good man who attacked a corrupt, legalistic system and was killed for it. Harry identified with that, as he often attacked corrupt systems and knew that people get crucified for it.

I have no doubt that Harry is alive today with God in whatever fashion our souls continue to exist with him. He didn't need to be saved in any Christian sense. In his case, that would have been clearly redundant. He was already a child of God.

SO WHAT DOES JESUS MEAN TO ME and how would I talk about him to a person who is not a Christian?

I came to my present understanding of the world and God through Jesus, or at least through the movement he inaugurated nearly two thousand years ago. Much of what I once believed because someone told me I should believe it I no longer find credible. And I am sure much of what I now believe is riddled with error. That is the nature of epistemological uncertainty — once we have seen our own tendency to get things wrong, we can never again be completely confident of our systems of belief.

The one thing of which I am *totally* confident, and on which I will stake my life, is the centrality of love, both in the teachings of Jesus and in the nature of the universe. My wife and I raised two sons; of all the things they have to know from their upbringing, the importance of love is uppermost. Until now, at least, neither has been acquisitive or materialistic, as many young people are. They care more about relationships and love and beauty than about anything else in the world. We all do. It is our credo, our commitment, our great hope in a world where it is difficult to know anything for certain.

What was the lovely saying with which Bishop John A. T. Robinson closed his little book *But That I Can't Believe!*? "The centre for the Christian is firm: the edges and the ends are gloriously and liberatingly open."[14]

I have always felt a little shortchanged, and maybe even

guilty, because I have never had a mystical experience of Jesus. I read the reports of those who have had near-death experiences, and how they have met Christ face-to-face, and I am frankly envious. I did see an angel when I was a late adolescent. I am convinced I did. It was the angel Gabriel, and he was as visible to me as Monica and Tess and Andrew are to the people in the TV program *Touched by an Angel,* only far more ethereal. That visit has meant more to me across the years than words can say. It has held my faith steady in many a gale. But I still feel a bit cheated not to have had a revelation from Jesus himself.

Maybe this is one reason I don't think it is necessary for people to have an experience with Christ in order to enter the kingdom of heaven. But the Jesus I read about in the Gospels is an amazingly transcendent figure — one who does change the lives of many who meet him, and whose ideas about God, life, and how we should live our lives have certainly revolutionized thinking about them, even among Jews, Muslims, Buddhists, and others. I accept that Jesus is the most extraordinary man who ever lived, and that God somehow, in a mystery, raised him from the dead. I cannot believe there would have been a Christianity or an early church if that incredible, miraculous event had not occurred. I have even overcome my fear of idolatry to actually worship Christ as my Lord, though for years I resisted this final step of commitment, thinking he would not have wanted it when he was an earthly teacher.

But I cannot for the life of me, after all these years of study and discipleship, believe that the Jesus of history or the Christ of faith would endorse a view limiting salvation to those who have publicly confessed him as their personal savior and are willing to follow him in the ritual of Christian baptism. I once preached a sermon called "The Wideness of Christ and the Narrowness of Christianity," and I am convinced that this matter demonstrates that disparity. Here

was a man whom the records show as an incredibly tolerant rabbi, open to Gentiles as well as Jews, to lepers and
tax collectors and whores and every other kind of social
outcast, who called as his disciples men who were as reli-
giously disinclined and unlikely as anybody could be, and
who died forgiving the very bigots and soldiers who put him
to death. I simply cannot believe that this man would have
any part in denying redemption to people who have never
heard his name, or even to people who know a great deal
about him but don't feel the need to announce that they
want to follow him.

As I have implied from the earliest pages of this book,
the literal mind is a very limited mind. I don't mean that
literalists are not smart; some I have known are extremely
clever and intelligent. But literalists lack the ability to see
beyond the names and images they think things have. It
doesn't occur to them to wonder how things happened to
be the way they are, or why we call them what we do, or to
pose the question of what things would be like if we simply
changed their names and knew them another way.

Rainer Maria Rilke once wrote a letter to a young friend
advising that if he ever became famous he should take another name, any name, so that God could call him in the
night. I wonder if God and Christ wouldn't sometimes like
to take other names and thus escape the excessive baggage
laid upon them by all the preachers and theologians of
the ages, especially the conservatives and fundamentalists.
Maybe Christ, in a playful mood, would choose "Buddha"
or "Mohammed" or "Confucius." Would the conservatives
say then, "You cannot come to God except by the Buddha
or the prophet Mohammed or the great ethicist Confucius"?

We take ourselves so seriously as knowers and thinkers.
Surely, after Plato's "Allegory of the Cave," we shouldn't be
so quick to think we have figured out the universe and the
world beyond. Or after the story of the blind men of Cathay,

who got hold of the elephant at different places and each had a unique description of what it was like, we shouldn't assume we understand everything there is to know about Jesus and salvation. Wouldn't it be more fitting for those who are supposed to "walk humbly with their God" to be a tad more tentative about their faith itself, and not to impose such rigid constructions on everything, including membership in the kingdom of heaven? It is simply unbecoming of Christians to behave so proprietarily with Christ, as if he belonged to us and not to the world at large.

Fourth Wrong Teaching

There Is No Salvation
Outside the (Conservative) Church

In the geography of my hometown, the church of a major denomination stood sentinel over each quadrant of the community. The First Baptist Church reigned over the area on North Main Street, one block from the town square. On South Main Street, two blocks from the square, was the First Christian Church (Disciples of Christ). Two blocks east of the square, on East Mount Vernon Street, stood the First Methodist Church. And one block west of the square, on West Columbia Street, was the First Presbyterian Church. That they were all named "first" something-or-other may have been a sign of early hopefulness in their respective denominations, though the Baptist church was the only one ever replicated within the city limits. And First Baptist Church was easily twice the size of the Methodist church, three times the size of the Christian church, and five times the size of the Presbyterian church.

The only African-American church I ever knew about was the African Methodist Episcopal, or A.M.E., which was located a block farther north from the Baptist church on Main Street, at the foot of a great hill where many of the town's finest homes stood watch over the entire community. I'm sure it was there to be near those homes, so that in the old days the Negro servants could attend church and return as soon as possible — though the services at the A.M.E. church were set for Sunday afternoon, after the dinner dishes had been cleared and washed at the big houses. There was a black Baptist church somewhere in the small back streets of the southeastern quadrant of town, but I can't remember having ever seen it.

The mammoth First Baptist Church obviously set the tone for life and worship in my small town, and everyone who belonged to it knew that. The pastor certainly knew it. He frequently dropped little asides in his sermons that indicated his awareness of the church's superiority. One of his favorite remarks, often repeated, concerned the houses in which the various ministers resided. "The Baptist preacher," he would say, "lives in a *pastorium*. The Methodist preacher lives in a *parsonage*. The Presbyterian preacher lives in a *manse*. And the Campbellite preacher [his slightly derisive term for the Christian Church, based on the name of Alexander Campbell, one of the founders of the Christian Church movement] lives wherever he can!" The term "pastorium" may have been of his own invention; I have not encountered it elsewhere.

I cannot speak for the other churches, but the members of First Baptist Church knew from both precept and innuendo that the unchurched members of our community were going to hell when they died. And we were always given the feeling that even those who attended the other churches stood in some danger of the same terrible fate unless God was in a particularly generous mood when they passed away.

We were kept aware of this dire situation by the annual — and sometimes biannual — revival meetings at our church, which were always times of intense prayer and supplication for the lost of the community. I often had the feeling that these "seasons of revival," as they were called, could be visualized as all-hands-on-deck times when floodlights were turned on the dark seas all around our great ship, sailing regally over the churning waters, and we church members were expected to spot people floundering in the waves and attempt their rescue.

For weeks before these meetings, our pastor would exhort us to pray for the lost. Sometimes so-called cottage prayer meetings would be organized for the success of the upcoming revival, and neighbors would gather to beseech the Lord for the souls of other, unchurched neighbors. During the revival meetings themselves, both the pastor and the visiting evangelist, and sometimes the visiting singer, would urge us daily to pray fervently for the lost and try to win them to Christ — that is, bring them to the church.

There were the obviously lost — people who attended no church at all. And there were the conceivably lost — those who attended the nonconservative churches. And as it often turned out, there were even a few lost in our church's own membership, who would come under conviction during a revival and make a new profession of faith in Christ, saying they had not really been saved the first time they joined the church. Almost every conservative church has at least one or two "repeat" joiners, who fulfill some inner need by being saved every time there is a successful revival.

For years, if someone said he or she was "lost," I thought immediately of that person's spiritual situation, not of the possibility that they were geographically challenged and trying to relocate themselves in relation to recognizable landmarks. And "finding Christ" was the antidote to being lost. Christ didn't find you; you somehow managed to find him. When we moved to Birmingham, Alabama, only a dozen years ago, my wife on her first visit to the supermarket was encountered by a woman carrying tracts who confronted her with the question, "Have you found Christ?" "I'm sorry," said my wife with an innocent look, "I didn't know he was lost."

A Baptist minister friend in Birmingham tells a story from his youth that illustrates this sociological phenomenon. He grew up in a town in northern Alabama where there was great rivalry between the Baptist church and the fundamentalist Church of Christ. During a revival meeting at the Baptist church, a member from the Church of Christ, a tall, thin, washed-out woman named Mrs. Wilson, was in attendance. My friend said he and some of his buddies usually sat behind her. She had the peculiar habit of sucking air through her teeth, so most nights he and his friends entertained themselves by counting the number of times she did this each minute. As the Baptist minister often quarreled in his sermons with Church of Christ theology, indicating that it was not truly adequate for salvation, most of the members of the Baptist church began to pray for Mrs. Wilson's conviction and salvation. At last, before the revival ended, Mrs. Wilson fell under conviction, as they say, and walked the aisle to confess her "new" faith in Christ and become a member of the Baptist church. There was great rejoicing in the congregation, and a sense of vindication for their theological position.

The Baptist pastor was so thrilled by Mrs. Wilson's conversion that he worked especially hard on a homily stating the obvious superiority of the Baptist doctrine of baptism over that of the Church of Christ, which he planned to give from the baptismal pool when he immersed Mrs. Wilson. At the big moment, placing a hand behind Mrs. Wilson's back and another over her nose, he plunged her beneath the water, beginning at the same time to deliver his sermon. It became obvious, however, that he had lost his hold on Mrs. Wilson and she was floundering under the water. Doggedly intent on delivering his sermon, the pastor continued speaking as he felt about for the baptismal candidate. Seconds passed. A minute. Still the pastor looked at the congregation, talking about baptism, and did not connect with Mrs. Wilson.

At last, a long, bony hand reached up and seized the thick glass at the front of the pool. Presently another hand appeared beside it. Mrs. Wilson hauled herself up and draped herself across the glass, her long hair, which had been pinned up, now cascading down below her. The pastor didn't miss a beat, but continued as before to deliver his sermon on the nature of Baptist baptism. As Mrs. Wilson did not move, but lay inertly across the edge of the baptistry, the congregation wondered if perhaps she had drowned in spite of her reappearance.

"We were relieved," said my friend, "when we heard her begin to suck air through her teeth again. But still the pastor did not acknowledge her resurrection from the watery depths. He kept right on smiling at the congregation and delivering that sermon."

I realize this story must sound to a non-Southerner like something straight out of Flannery O'Connor. But those who have been reared in conservative churches, especially in the South, will recognize its authenticity. Most of us could tell other stories just as improbable-sounding and swear they really happened. I repeat this one not only because it is amusing but because it illustrates so vividly the sharp distinction made in conservative churches between the lost and the saved, and the strong conviction among their members that people outside their congregations are literally beyond the boundaries of divine grace.

THIS CONVICTION among conservative religious people that theirs is the only church in which salvation is a sure thing lends great impetus to evangelism. Liberal Christians don't have a passion for the lost because they aren't really certain anybody is lost. If God is a loving deity and hell is only a mythological idea from a more benighted time, there is not much to save people from except suffering and ignorance in this life. So liberals busy themselves with voter registration, slum reclamation, disease control, ecological concerns, and the quality of education, while conservatives worry about getting everybody into their own particular churches.

There was a bestselling religious book a few years ago by Dean M. Kelley called *Why Conservative Churches Are Growing*.[15] Kelley, an attorney, was puzzled by the statistics being reported to the National Council of Churches, showing that membership in the NCC's support churches was declining while national church attendance was soaring. What was going on? Kelley's research demonstrated that conservative churches knew who they were (God's chosen people) and what they needed to do (win the lost) and were willing to expend every effort to achieve their goals. Liberal churches, on the other hand, were often vague about their theology and did not bother to articulate any plan of member recruitment.

There certainly was no lack of understanding in my home church of our role in the community or our calling to save everybody in it. I still cringe at the memory of my first experience as a soul-winner. I was sixteen, and was deputized, along with a twenty-year-old friend, to call on a young laborer who was known to have no church relationship. Pumped up by a previsitation prayer meeting, my friend and I drove to the apartment building where the young man and his wife lived. We climbed the steps and rapped on their door. It was only eight o'clock, but they were already in bed, as the young man's work required that he rise quite early. He appeared at the door somewhat dazed, obviously having been asleep. He had pulled on his jeans but was otherwise unclothed.

There in the doorway, beneath the light of a naked bulb, I talked to him about his soul and the biblical plan of salvation as I had learned it. My friend, though older, was much shyer and remained silent. The young man, instead of being angry with us, was extremely polite and appeared grateful that we had come. He admitted that he had often thought he ought to become a Christian and join the church, but he'd never been asked. We had a prayer together, he accepted Jesus, we shook his hand and sent him back to bed, we reported his name to the church, the pastor called on him and arranged for his presentation to the congregation, and he was baptized within a week.

By the time I went off to Baylor University the next fall, therefore, I was a veteran soul-winner and eagerly joined a group of devout students who went off campus each Friday night to conduct street missions in the riverfront area of Waco, Texas, where migrant workers gathered on weekends to drink and forget their troubles. We had a little portable organ, played hymns, preached to passersby, handed out tracts, and "counseled" with any of the workers who would stop to talk with us. It was a tough area, and there were always three or four fights on a Friday evening, the night when most of the workers were paid. Once I saw a drunken man kicking his girlfriend's head against a curb. I learned not to take any money with me when I went to the mission, as I always met many people down on their luck to whom I would give it. Then, as soon as they got a dollar or two, they headed straight back to the nearest bar.

Now that I have grown older and wiser — and more liberal — I regard our street-front mission in that bowery district as the futile engagement of foolish hearts. What could a bunch of WASP students from a Christian university bring to a population of largely illiterate cowboys, bean-pickers, and derrick-hands? We were all Don Quixotes tilting at the windmills of evil. I doubt if a single one of the "conversions" we chalked up over the years ever held, or a single bit of advice we proffered about straightening up or getting married or going to Alcoholics Anonymous ever did an iota of real good.

What I have gleaned from those early experiences, though, is an understanding of the heart and mind of conservatives and fundamentalists about the meaning of church and the importance of throwing out the lifeline to the lost. Many of them pay only lip service to the ideal, but the ideal itself is powerful. And it is what continues to fuel the membership growth of conservative churches, whether they are part of older denominations or belong to the vanguard of newer, independent, megachurches around the country.

ALTHOUGH I THINK THE TREND is waning a little now, the strong sense of denominational identity among Southern Baptists, Assemblies of God, Church of Christ, and other conservative groups has long impelled their members, whenever they move, quickly to unite with another church of the same brand. Nowhere is this practice more evident than in college and university towns, where the large influx of students in late August or early September results in massive receptions of new members.

Baylor University is the largest Baptist institution of higher learning in the world. When I went there in 1950, there were between four and five thousand students. Now there must be five times that many. In 1950, there were four major Baptist churches — First Baptist, Seventh and James, Highland, and Columbus Avenue — that garnered most of the new-membership trade. Many in the student body were so fastidious about church membership that they actually took theirs home for the summer and brought it back again at the beginning of the fall term. Thus there were probably three thousand students changing their church membership in any given season.

As the business of moving back to the college churches usually took a month or six weeks each fall, invitation time in the Sunday service — when the doors of church membership were opened — during those weeks was like a great, rowdy revival meeting, with hundreds of students streaming down the aisles to be greeted by the beaming pastor and get reentered on the local roll. And, as many students proved somewhat fickle about this resettling process, often changing churches once or twice as they met new friends on campus, broke up with old sweethearts, or simply found that the worship in another church was more agreeable than that in the one they had chosen, they kept circulating among the major churches all year, as if they were playing religious musical chairs.

Growth statistics for these churches were usually staggering, as they seldom reported the downsizings that occurred just as frequently, and there was always a sense of euphoria in the air as waves of new students returned in the fall. A friend and former student of mine once pastored one of these churches, and told me the administration of such an organization was a roller-coaster experience, with everything rising to great heights when the students were there, then dipping equally low when they deserted in the summers. The Baptist churches in the city, he confessed, were in frightful financial condition, as most students gave very little money to the maintenance of the institution and some of the largest, most outwardly prosperous congregations had to depend on the generosity of a small cadre of devoted resident families to keep them going at all.

When I was a freshman at Baylor, I joined First Baptist Church because I was caught up in the fever of the crowd joining the Sunday I was there. Later, as winter approached and the distance to First Baptist proved formidable because I did not have a car and could not afford bus fare several times a week, I began attending Seventh and James, which was just across the street from the campus, and I soon transferred my membership there. When my wife and I married and moved to Waco at the beginning of my senior year, we joined Columbus Avenue Baptist Church, which was across town. We then had a car and wanted to get as far away from the hordes of unmarried students as possible, and we liked the elderly pastor, W. W. Melton, who was in the habit of preaching a rather short sermon, closing his Bible, and saying, "I've already told you more than you will remember. It's time to sing a hymn and go home."

Now, almost half a century and several denominations later, my wife and I are still nagged in our consciences about church membership. I pastor a small resort church on an island off the coast of Michigan in the summertime, and we are both members of that congregation. Back home in Virginia, we visit several churches in our community, trying to snuggle down and feel comfortable enough in one particular church to join it for the remainder of the year. Thus far we have not been successful in finding such a church, and it troubles us. Raised with a sense of urgency about church membership, we shall probably be haunted all our lives by a need to belong and to feel that the church where we are members is part of our process of redemption. Only now we know enough about churches and their collective mindsets to be wary of them.

RUBEM ALVES, THE BRAZILIAN THEOLOGIAN, said in *Tomorrow's Child* that if one wanted to predict where Jesus would go in any modern city, were he living now, it would be possible to determine the possibilities by shading only two areas of the city map: first would be the parks and wooded scenes, where he would go to pray and be alone with the Father; and second would be the areas of specific pain in the city, such as the hospitals, the jails, the ghettos, and the public schools.[16]

One of the shortcomings of the conservative church is its focus on the value of church membership to those on the inside and its almost total neglect of the mission of the church to those who live in constant pain. Conservatism in this country, ever since the arrival of the Puritans in New England, has talked and dreamed so exclusively of heaven and the life after death that it has tended to ignore the enormous social problems that exist right under its nose, some of them even spawned by the greed and selfishness of its members. It has always placed more emphasis on belonging to the church and being counted among the elect than on specific ways in which members should be involved in relieving the ills of society around them. Thus a conservative church could countenance slavery for many years and ignore the evils of the industrial revolution that made so many of its members wealthy. And today it can take comfort in its celebrity status in this country without concerning itself about the poverty of immigrant groups, the breakdown of interracial dialogue, or the poisoning of the environment.

Looking back on my early days at First Baptist Church in my hometown, I realize what an exquisite drama was being played out between the church fathers and a frail-looking old woman who came back home from the mission fields in China because World War II had broken out. Her name was Miss Anna Clark. Everybody emphasized the "Miss," as it seemed part of her saintliness, along with her years of missionary work and her obvious devotion to God. Miss Anna was horrified, when she returned home, to find a number of families living in wretched squalor on a narrow little lane called Vine Street, only a few hundred yards from the historic old town square. The offending part of Vine Street was only one long block, but it was lined with tiny, unpainted hovels, many of them with no plumbing or electricity, where in the summer hordes of dirty children ran about in various states of near-nudity. Most of the little houses were owned by a prominent businessman. There was no drug problem at that time — the poor denizens of this ghetto could not have supported a dealer, even with help from the federal government — but the area was a breeding-ground for crime, as marital arrangements were extremely loose and none of the inhabitants had anything to lose if they were caught stealing and went to prison.

One Sunday during a revival meeting, Miss Anna, a fastidi-
ously clean little woman with thinning white hair, who always
wore an oversized straw hat out in the sunlight, walked forward with those offering their repentance and joining the
church, and asked the pastor's permission to say a word to
the congregation. The pastor, imagining she wanted to offer
her testimony, relinquished his pulpit. Then Miss Anna, in a
quiet voice and with great earnestness on her face, launched
into a speech about the appalling conditions she had cata-
logued on Vine Street and called upon the congregation to
join her in a crusade to set them right.

The effect was as if a bomb had fallen on First Baptist
Church. Once the debris settled, there was absolute silence.
No one knew what to do about Miss Anna's concern. To
the pastor and the congregation, her interest seemed as foreign as the inlands of China where she had once labored.
This was a church where people got saved, not a social-
reclamation institution. Surely there were agencies in the
community to take care of any problems she had discovered on Vine Street — the county health authorities, for
example — and it was completely inappropriate for anything
like this to be brought up at a revival meeting where souls
were being rescued from the ravages of sin.

The pastor mumbled some word of appreciation to Miss
Anna for her concern and promptly ignored what she had
said, trying to redirect everybody's attention to the fine
ingathering of the lost and reclamation of errant church
members who had come to transfer their membership from
sister churches in other towns. After church, Miss Anna was
lost in the shuffle of the congregation to greet the saved and
reclaimed, and aside from the gossiping that surely went on
for several days about "that poor, demented old saint," the
effect of what she had done was totally lost.

But Miss Anna was not faint of heart. Not a woman who
had gone as a slip of a girl to cast her lot as a missionary

in the Far East and had labored for years as a teacher on a salary that barely kept her in rice and sunbonnets. She first set about getting medical assistance for some of the children on Vine Street suffering from malnutrition and various effects of it. Then she began badgering business-men in the community for money to improve the sanitation and comfort of the little houses. She must have made the man who owned them extremely uncomfortable, for wher-ever she went she complained to others of the unsalutary conditions in which his tenants lived. She undertook the education of the adults who lived on beggars' row, teaching the illiterate to read and indoctrinating parents in the mys-teries of personal hygiene and financial management. And before she was through with her project, several years later, some of the least worthy houses had been demolished, many of the families had been relocated to better homes, and Vine Street looked like a park compared to its earlier appearance.

First Baptist Church, however, for all its power and wealth as the largest church in the community, didn't turn a hand to help with the transformation. Once or twice, the congre-gation voted in its regular business sessions, at Miss Anna's behest, to divert a few hundred dollars to specific needs she had identified, but that was only hush money, or perhaps even guilt money. But for the most part everybody just stood by and watched Miss Anna clean up the town's only slum, and I expect everybody wondered what motivated her to do it. We were all going to die, after all, whether we lived on Main Street hill or on lower Vine Street, and it was the dis-position of our eternal souls that was really important, not the condition of the real estate around us.

Half a century later, when I returned for First Baptist Church's celebration of its two-hundredth anniversary, I didn't think things had changed very much. The church had built a beautiful new sanctuary only a few yards from the old one. It isn't much larger than the old one, though it does enjoy better lighting and a much more sophisticated sound system, and it is wheelchair accessible without the use of an elevator, which was required in the older building. I'm sure it cost several million dollars. Vine Street has remained pretty much as it was when Miss Anna completed her work there, and the community doesn't have any other obvious slums. But I feel rather certain there are some students who could use help with their college tuition, and I actually know some people who can't afford the medication they need because it costs more than their monthly pensions and medical insurance will allow. I have heard of some elderly people who subsist part of the month on pet food because their Social Security payments don't begin to cover their requirements.

When I preached for the anniversary celebration, I talked about how the spirit of the Lord is always coming freshly on old congregations, and what mixed privileges and responsibilities that entails. But I seriously doubt if anything has changed in the way the church does its business. It is, after all, engaged in the task of preaching the good news of Jesus and trying to save the town's citizens to eternal life. Anything more is left to the government and other charitable agencies.

THE PRIDE CONSERVATIVE AND FUNDAMENTALIST churches feel in themselves and their missions is a great stumbling block to church unity and ecumenical relations in our time. Liberal churches are not great either, and too easily write off their conservative counterparts as being too much trouble or not worth the effort when it comes to establishing coalitions for greater dialogue and more effective cooperation in the community. But the conservative churches of my experience think they have the truth and don't want to be contaminated by association with congregations that don't think exactly as they do.

I can't remember a single ecumenical gathering of churches in my hometown when I was a boy. The only ecumenical thing that ever happened was a wedding or a funeral, and even those special occasions in a small town tended to be more intrachurch than not. The high school commencement, held on Sunday evenings, was of course interdenominational; but I can remember years when the Baptist church refused to cancel its Sunday-night service so its members could attend. Our church was the only one large enough to sponsor a gathering of the various congregations, and I am sure it never occurred to anybody in a leadership position — certainly not the pastor or the deacons — to invite any non-Baptists to join us for anything except a revival meeting, when it was hoped some of them would see the light and make a real confession of faith.

The A.M.E. church down the street had a great soloist named Pansy West, who was as big and bosomy as a diva, and our pastor loved to hear her sing. Pansy occasionally got drunk at the Newtonian Hotel, where she worked in the kitchen, and guests could hear her singing at the top of her voice. Twice that I can recall, our pastor asked Pansy to sing for our congregation at a Sunday-evening service. But I cannot remember that he ever invited other members of her church to accompany her, or even her immediate family members. It was daring enough to have Pansy come by herself.

When I was a pastor in Lynchburg, Virginia, and later in Los Angeles, California, I remember that few Southern Baptists and other conservatives ever attended the ecumenical ministers' gatherings. Jerry Falwell never came to interfaith meetings in Lynchburg. In the Wilshire District of Los Angeles, where we had an organization to feed the hungry and another to promote literacy among the thousands of immigrants pouring into our area every year, there was splendid cooperation from Jewish rabbis, Roman Catholic priests, and ministers of the large Nazarene and American Baptist churches in the neighborhood. But no Southern Baptists participated.

Every year, our church, First Congregational, sponsored an ecumenical Thanksgiving service. We planned the liturgy with the other ministers of the area, and had wonderful attendance from all the churches in the Wilshire District. When the Christian flag went down the long center aisle with the American flag, so did the Jewish Torah. When the great Tom Bradley was mayor of Los Angeles, he always came for the service, so we began calling it the Mayor's Thanksgiving Service. But to our sorrow, no one from the conservative churches ever came. They knew they wouldn't hear the right catchwords and phrases in the sermon — especially if it was delivered by a Catholic or a Jew.

My saddest story as a former Baptist takes me back to January 25, 1973, the day the war in Vietnam officially ended. I was at Fuchu Air Force Base in Tokyo, with Father Eugene Schallert of San Francisco University, to lead a seminar for Air Force chaplains. There were about thirty of us in the group, including several chaplains flown in from Vietnam. When news of the peace accord reached us from Saigon, we all felt an enormous surge of emotion. Someone suggested that we have a thanksgiving Communion service to conclude our seminar. One of the chaplains went to the Officers' Mess to get some bread and wine, while Father Schallert and I planned the liturgy. We asked a Jewish chaplain named Morton Levine, who styled himself "Chief Rabbi of All Thailand," as he was the only Jewish chaplain there, to participate by giving a brief meditation over the bread and cup, and he was thrilled to do so. Instead of a homily, we passed an embrace around the group and then asked each chaplain to say a few words about how he was feeling. I'll never forget the outpouring of thanksgiving among those chaplains. But some also spoke of fear, particularly for the ones returning to Vietnam. We knew they would be the last removed from that strife-torn country. If the North Vietnamese swarmed into Saigon before the final helicopter had left, one or two of them might well be captured and executed. Having Communion under these conditions was unspeakably moving.

But then two Southern Baptist chaplains and one from the Missouri Synod Lutherans refused to accept the bread and wine. One Baptist said he wouldn't drink wine. The other said he believed in "closed Communion" — something to be taken only in one's local church. The MSL chaplain said he wasn't allowed to receive Communion outside his own denomination. Father Schallert and I regarded them in disbelief. How could anybody, in the excitement of a time like that, refuse to join Christian brothers in remembering the death of Christ and celebrating his presence among us?

If I had still been a Southern Baptist at that time, I would have left the denomination in disgust.

IT ISN'T ANY WONDER God's people are so hopelessly splintered here on earth. There simply isn't enough love to bring us together and to obliterate our differences of doctrine and understanding. Maybe in heaven it will be better.

The longer I live, the more I understand Simone Weil, the Alsatian philosopher who became a Christian in the first half of the nineteenth century. Although she professed her faith in Christ and dedicated her life to following him, she refused to join a church, because she said it would separate her from some of her friends whom she dearly loved.

It is a shame that belonging to any church could ever separate anybody from people in the world who don't belong. Jesus wanted love and unity above everything else, and he preached it to his disciples. But apparently it isn't such a big priority with us. We forget that the Gospel of John says "God so loved the *world* that he sent his only Son," not "God so loved the *church*," etc. The world and its needs ought to come first, and we ought to be able to unite around those, even if we have difficulty loving one another.

But we are still human, and in many ways untransformed, so we have different ideas of what the church ought to be and how it ought to behave. How many years was it after Jesus' death that the early church had a serious split between the way Peter viewed things and the way Paul saw them? Sadly, not very many.

Fifth Wrong Teaching

Worship Is Proclamation before It Is Anything Else

In the church where I grew up, worship basically meant listening to preaching. Of the hour between eleven and twelve on Sunday morning, thirty minutes was regularly reserved for the sermon. Often it ran to thirty-five or forty minutes. When people talked about going to worship, they said they were going to preaching. "Were you at preaching last Sunday?" We never said worship. It was always preaching.

Everything else we did in a religious service — singing hymns, listening to solos or anthems, praying, having announcements, reading the Scriptures — was known as "the preliminaries." They didn't actually exist in their own right, but as a prelude to the really important thing, the proclamation of the Word. Even the reading of Scriptures was subsumed under preaching, for it was always the preacher's choice of a text for his sermon, not a text from the lectionary to be heard on its own.

It is no wonder, therefore, that Billy Graham, by all odds the best known preacher in the history of the world, excepting perhaps Jesus and the Apostles, was a product of Southern Baptist churches. He was shaped by the Southern Baptist preaching tradition, which always treated religious music, prayer, and the reading of the Bible as "warm-ups" for the preacher, to get the crowd (and maybe even the preacher) in the mood to hear the voice of God speaking to them through the words of the minister.

There was never a question, in a Southern Baptist church, about where the pulpit should go. It was always set smack-dab in the middle of everything, where the preacher had the clearest vision possible of everybody in the sanctuary except the choir behind him, and where everybody could see him to the very best advantage. And it wasn't long after electricity came into church buildings that Baptists began rigging up spotlights to shine on the preacher, so that the house lights could be dimmed and everything else faded into the background to magnify the preaching of the Word.

It was a Baptist preacher visiting Westminster Abbey who once proclaimed, "I can see why this old church died and had to be turned into a museum. They put the pulpit off to the side where half the people can't even see it!"

Baptists and other conservative groups have an oratorical tradition all their own that is quite different, say, from that of the Presbyterians, which descends through great Scottish preachers such as Ian Maclaren, A. J. Gossip, and James Stewart. It usually includes having a very simple outline that is more emotional than intellectual, stating the obvious as cleverly as possible, saying it in a variety of tones and emphases, lacing everything with humor, and closing with a memorable story or poem. In the last fifty years, stories have been much favored over poems. The language is plain and forthright, the voicing firm and authoritative, and the pacing varied enough to impart style or maintain interest. The Bible is used primarily to provide legitimacy for the main thesis being propounded, and the sermon often uses the text merely as a jumping-off place, not as an object of study or analysis.

This is a tradition derived from frontier days, when an itinerant preacher arrived in a community, announced a meeting, had a few hymns to warm up the crowd, and launched into a peroration designed to bring sinners to the altar or the weeping bench. In most conservative contexts, such a preaching style is more successful if it is not too subtle and merely restates in attractive form what the people already know and believe.

Conservative churches have a kind of star system enfolding their preachers. All the pastors know who the big preachers are, follow their careers, imitate their preaching, and invite them to hold meetings in their churches.

Several years ago I preached in the church of a minister who said he had been W. A. Criswell's roommate at Baylor University. Criswell was the legendary old fundamentalist who followed the great George W. Truett as senior minister of the First Baptist Church of Dallas, Texas. This minister said that Criswell had arrived first at the dorm room they were assigned to share, and when he got there Criswell had already commandeered the best pieces of furniture and the largest share of storage space. When he entered the room, he said, young Criswell was standing before a mirror declaiming one of George Truett's sermons. Criswell offered no apologies; he was unashamed of being caught imitating the famous preacher. "I'm going to be pastor of First Baptist Dallas some day," promised Criswell. And he molded himself into the kind of pulpit orator who could do it.

ONCE, WHEN WALTER WAGGONER was still head of the Fund for Theological Education, I participated with him and a committee of about a dozen people in a study of courses in worship and spirituality at seminaries across the U.S. We were amazed to find that there were no such courses in the conservative and fundamentalist seminaries. There were plenty of courses in preaching, but none in the context in which preaching is normally done. All the Southern Baptist seminaries, in fact — six of them — had whole departments of preaching, and even offered doctoral programs in that subject. But none saw any need for training ministers in the art of designing or leading in liturgy.

The free-church movement has of course always been somewhat antiliturgical, especially in Britain and America. And given the development of most conservative churches in the frontier spirit of this country, many free churches have an abhorrence of written prayers and responses — elements of worship they consider "popish" and high church. In the church where I grew up, for example, such prayers would have been considered grossly insincere. God looks on the heart, our pastor would have said, not on fine syntax. Consequently we heard the same prayers every Sunday, or at least the same phrases and petitions recycled, varied only according to the person praying.

My home church claimed not to have a liturgy — again, that was too Catholic — but its pattern of worship was as set as any liturgy in Christendom. As I recall it, it went like this: Choral Introit, Opening Hymn, Prayer, Hymn, Welcome, Announcements, Offering, Prayer, Special Music (solo or anthem), Sermon, Invitation and Invitation Hymn, Benediction. The pastor usually called on one of the deacons to give the first prayer, gave the prayer at the offering himself, and called on Brother Dodson, chairman of the board of deacons, for the benediction.

Brother Dodson, a tall, elderly insurance salesman with a wife as short and stout as he was thin and lanky, always carried his hat into the sanctuary and slid it under the seat he occupied. As he grew older, he also had a habit of nodding off during the sermon. When the pastor called on him to give the benediction, his wife gently nudged him in the ribs. At her prodding, he would bend down, retrieve his hat, stand with everyone else, pronounce a brief benediction, put on his hat, and quit the sanctuary.

I was sitting behind the Dodsons one Sunday morning when the pastor decided to vary this routine and call on Brother Dodson to give the prayer at the offering. Brother Dodson had already dozed off. His wife touched him in the ribs, a bit vigorously, I thought. He started, reached down for his hat, stood, pronounced a benediction, and proceeded into the aisle with his little wife grabbing for his coattail.

That happened to be one Sunday when there was a little variety in the service, but the variety did not extend to the order of the liturgy itself.

ALTHOUGH BROTHER DODSON'S PRAYERS were rather phlegmatic, the free-church system did produce some rather eloquent public *prayers*. We had prayer meeting every Wednesday evening in my boyhood, an hour that consisted of singing several old favorite hymns of the sort we didn't use on Sunday morning (I now realize they were holdovers from the old folks' childhoods, such as "Bringing in the Sheaves" and "Sweet Hour of Prayer"), hearing a report on the shut-ins and people in the hospital, declaring "a season of prayer" for them, and listening to the pastor render a Bible study of a rather informal nature, indicating he had prepared differently for this than he did for his sermons on Sunday.

The pastor would normally call on two or three laymen to pray during the "season of prayer," and in the relaxed atmosphere of this evening service they often seemed to "cut loose" and offer extremely fervent prayers. Dr. Robert Jasper, who had briefly studied for the ministry and had worked as a medical missionary in the mountains of eastern Kentucky during the years when that region was as primitive as any region of the Congo, was one of the most rhetorical of these laymen, and his loud, resonant voice appeared to assault the very gates of heaven itself. I can't remember any of his prayers well enough to attempt a reconstruction of one, but I do recall admiring some of the phrases he employed, as they were of the grand, sonorous style I then found attractive in a volume of the speeches of old Governor Bob Taylor of Tennessee, which I had somehow acquired.

There was a kind of unction in such prayers, and for several years as a young minister I attempted to achieve it in my own pulpit prayers. As I never attended any church but the Baptist church, I did not encounter written prayers from the lectern or pulpit until I went off to Harvard Divinity School, where *nobody* would have had the temerity to offer public prayer without having crafted it very carefully in advance. Some of these prayers, I had to admit, were very neatly done, and expressed their concerns with great articulateness, but I usually had the feeling that they were somewhat deficient in sincerity and passion.

Dr. George Arthur Buttrick, my professor of preaching and church leadership, struck me as a rather queer little fellow. He was quite eminent — *pre*eminent, even — by Eastern establishment standards. He had been pastor of renowned Madison Avenue Presbyterian Church in New York City for nearly three decades, had written several widely known books, had served as moderator of the United Presbyterian Church, had edited the prestigious multivolume *Interpreter's Bible,* and was now Preacher to Harvard University. As I listened to his quavering voice in the lectures and beheld his nervous, fidgety way of delivering them, I wondered how far he would have gotten as a Southern Baptist. He would probably not have gone beyond some remote, county-seat church with such a peculiar style and a heavy dependence on notes and written materials.

"If you have only a couple of hours for preparation," Buttrick urged us in his intense, comical manner, "spend them on the prayers for Sunday morning instead of the sermon."

I don't imagine *he* ever preached a sermon that had not been given its full ten or fifteen hours (or in the case of his Harvard sermons, twenty or thirty), and this sounded absolutely heretical to me. But a couple of years later, when I had become Dean of the Chapel at Georgetown College in Kentucky, I began carefully preparing each of the prayers

I employed, including even the benedictions. And before long I had become so addicted to the method, and so convinced it was the only responsible way of leading worship for several hundred people at a time, that I would never again undertake a Sunday service without having striven beforehand with the angels of public prayer.

Some older students at the college — veterans on the G.I. bill already pastoring rural churches — complained about these "unspiritual" prayers, for they regarded them the way I regarded the ones I heard at Harvard. But my officemate in the English department, Dr. Ralph Curry, a passionate, witty man, always leapt to my defense. "For God's sake," he half-shouted at one of the complainers, "you even make a list before you go to the grocery store. Don't you think God Almighty deserves more?"

ONCE I RECEIVED A LETTER from one of disgruntled conservatives in the student audience at the college. It said simply, "Sir, you are not a Christian." It was signed — just as simply — "A Christian."

Among many Baptist churches, I am happy to say, the prejudice against written prayers has been greatly modified over the years, and a number of my minister friends now work very hard on the ideas and phrasing of their prayers before getting into the pulpit on Sunday. But they are still very much in the minority. I seldom hear a prayer, when I am visiting in a conservative church, that shows any attention to forethought and careful articulation.

Why should conservative pastors give forethought to their prayers when many don't even give very much thought to their sermons? There is a joke I have sometimes told at ministers' gatherings about three ministers — a Presbyterian, a United Methodist, and a Baptist — who were out in a boat fishing at noon on Saturday. "Hey, fellows," suddenly exclaimed the Presbyterian, "I've got to get home. I haven't finished my sermon for tomorrow!" "Oh, wow!" said the Methodist, "you're right. I haven't even started mine." "Well, all right," said the Baptist grudgingly, "we'll go if you have to. But what do you fellows do during the anthem on Sunday morning?"

SØREN KIERKEGAARD said that we are accustomed, when we worship, to behaving as if God is on stage and we are arrayed around him like patrons at the theater. But the truth of the matter is that *we* are the actors on stage when we worship, and God is the audience. The liturgist and the preacher are actually the prompters in this case — they whisper to the worshipers what they should be doing and saying in order to please the observing deity.

Conservative churches and their ministers don't seem to understand this. For them, with their central pulpits and their emphasis on evangelism, it is the preacher, first and foremost, who is on stage, and perhaps a song leader and a choir, and in the case of TV churches and a few more theatrical churches, a celebrity figure singing a song or giving a testimony. Since frontier days and jackanapes ministers like Billy Sunday, these churches and ministers have confused *entertainment* with worship, and have been more interested in crowd-pleasing than in truly helping people come before God in all his love and holiness.

I strongly fear that the megachurches and metachurches of America have enshrined this cheaper philosophy of worship at the heart of their enterprise. The word "enterprise" is a key. They are almost all of an entrepreneurial nature — have had to be — because they are building something from scratch and not depending on the largesse of a denominational group or some other funding agency to get started. The bottom line of what they must do is attract and entertain crowds, so that people will continue to come to their churches and get involved in their programs.

In the planning sessions preceding their public gatherings, therefore, the staffs of these churches concentrate on creating "liturgies" and programs that will appeal to the largest numbers of people. This means neutering the prayers and sermons (and even the hymns) of controversial references and unpopular theological stances, and above all creating an environment of warmth and acceptance in which those who come will feel welcome and encouraged. Songs and anthems must be simple and upbeat and should have a strong emotional appeal. The use of the Bible is very tricky. There must be enough Scripture and orthodox exposition to reassure people of God's involvement. Yet there must not be too much Scripture, as people find it easily remote and boring, and it must not create a forbidding or critical atmosphere.

And Communion — oh, that is a sad story! Communion is not regarded in most conservative churches as entertaining, and it has been axed from the worship experience. Baptism is considered happy and uplifting, whether it is the baptism of infants with the beaming young parents and godparents gathered around the font, or the triumphant emergence of believers from the experience of total immersion. Baptism conveniently symbolizes new life, personal transformation, eternal hope, and is therefore adjudged photogenic, good press, positive vibes, reinforcing the image these churches want to convey. But Communion, on the other hand, is a downer. It remembers Jesus' death and invites meditation. It permits too much undirected time and allows people's thoughts to wander.

When Dr. Jim Henry, president of the Southern Baptist Convention and pastor of a vast church in Orlando, Florida, spoke to a pastors' conference at Samford University in the early 1990s, he was very blunt about Communion. "It is best not to have it at all," he said. "Or if you must have it, don't announce that you're going to. Sneak it in on a Sunday that isn't too important anyway. Serve it quickly and get it over."

Consider the poor Episcopalian, Lutheran, and Roman Catholic churches saddled with Communion every Sunday. And the Christian Church (Disciples of Christ), for whom weekly Communion has been an article of liturgical faith from the beginning of the denomination in the nineteenth century. Maybe the frequency of Communion is one reason for the terrible slump in Disciple membership over the last fifty years. Their decline is so heavy that the denomination commissioned a five-year study and produced a massive collection of documents about their losses. The recurrent theme in the reports was that ministers of the denomination were out of touch with the mainstream of the membership. Educated primarily at Yale and Vanderbilt, they tended to be more liberal than their constituents and more interested in social problems than in orthodox expressions of faith. But I can't help thinking that having Communion every Sunday has actually had more to do with the declining membership than anything else. If the majority of Disciples are conservatives, as the reports suggest, they may well be like other conservatives, who find Communion nonentertaining and therefore disinviting.

WHEN I WAS A PASTOR in Lynchburg, Virginia, I sometimes hosted Baptist ministers from the community, at their request, in luncheon meetings where they could air their grievances without their church members accidentally overhearing. Primarily they needed to talk about the pain they were enduring because of the apparent "success" of Jerry Falwell's Thomas Road Baptist Church and its various ministries. As I had once been a Baptist, they knew I would sympathize with their plight; and as I had been openly critical of Falwell, they knew they could speak their minds about him and the conservativism he represented.

The most galling thing these ministers had to endure, they said, was constant complaints from their church members that the worship in their churches was not as interesting and entertaining as the TV programs from Thomas Road Baptist Church. "Why can't we have bigger choirs and some better singers like they do?" "Why don't we ever get any celebrities to come to our church and give their testimonies?" Or even more personal: "I wish our preacher would take a stand on more things the way Rev. Falwell does. He really knows the Bible and tells it like it is!"

One minister said he only wished his members understood the part that busing played in Thomas Road's success. "Jerry was smart," he said, "to get all those old school buses and send them all over the county to pick up people. Now they run clear down to Roanoke in one direction and halfway to Richmond in the other direction, and they give rewards to the bus drivers who bring in the most new people every Sunday!"

I had not heard about the "rewards." Apparently I was the only one in the room who didn't know, and they all fell over one another in responding. One remembered a week when there was a big motorcycle — he didn't know if it was a Honda or a Harley — on a platform outside Thomas Road Church, and that it was designated as a gift for the driver who brought in the most visitors that month.

"Hell, it isn't just the church," said another minister, "it's the drivers themselves. With gifts and cash incentives at stake, they turn around and offer enticements to the people who come to church. One of them gives out free guppies to the children. Another uses candy bars. Some of them even give out free movie tickets, even though Falwell says they shouldn't go to the movies!"

And God is in the audience when we worship. It is a daunting thought.

I'VE BEEN REVIEWING the things I've written here and feeling a little guilty. I realize, in spite of my Harvard and Princeton education and my bias now for written prayers and prepared sermons, that I still want people to feel good about having been in worship — that I would have somehow failed them if I didn't send them away feeling mystically inspired and personally encouraged to hitch themselves up and put a little more effort into their spiritual quests.

Maybe this is why I am always conscious, when I am writing my sermon manuscripts, to lighten up now and then when I have been too heavy, or to inject a little wit or humor when it seems appropriate. I am better about this than I used to be. When I was a young preacher still under the strong influence of my conservative background, I didn't flinch at telling jokes in a sermon, or sometimes in the service itself, especially during the announcements. I had grown up hearing jokes from the pulpit and thought it was the way you kept people interested in the service.

I attended a Baptist church recently and heard the assistant minister tell a rather long, involved joke during the service. I cringed, remembering the days when I would have done such a thing. It seemed to me now strongly incompatible with the worship of God — something tossed in gratuitously to produce a moment of levity in an otherwise tedious hour.

Speaking of "incompatible," I'll never forget returning to my home church during my days in graduate school to hear a famous revivalist named Angel Martinez preach. Angel was something else. A poor Mexican immigrant who had somehow managed to attend Baylor University, where he left a reputation for having a photographic memory, Angel had parlayed his sultry good looks, a gift for theatrical speech and gestures, and a penchant for flashy clothes into a stellar career as an itinerant evangelist. He enjoyed explaining his passion for wild clothes — yellow sports jackets and purple slacks, in a day when all ministers wore either navy blue or black — by recalling how desperately poor he was as a boy. "I had no shoes, and I used to look at the other boys with their shoes and think, 'Boy, when I grow up, I am going to make a lot of money, and I am going to have the prettiest clothes that money can buy!' "

People loved it.

Angel also had an addiction to fancy cars, and reportedly owned several at a time. Once he telephoned a minister in a mill town where he was engaged to preach the following week and said, "Brother So-and-so, it just occurred to me that maybe I should call you. I was planning to drive over next week in my pretty blue Cadillac, but then I got to thinking, I'll bet those people are mostly Ford and Chevrolet people and they wouldn't understand my having a Cadillac. Am I right?" The minister said that he was. "I knew it," said Angel. "I'll come in my little car." The minister thanked him profusely for being so sensitive. The next week, Angel arrived in a purple Jaguar.

The time I returned home to hear him speak, I was late getting to the church. The "preliminaries" of music, prayer, and offering were over, and Angel was on. I tiptoed into the narthex, where an overflow crowd was sitting in folding chairs. One of the deacons shook my hand and pulled forward another chair for me. The crowd was rocking with laughter. I sat and listened. What I heard was one funny story after another, some of them sexually suggestive. People were cracking up. There was an aura of the convention crowd about the place.

When Angel finally recited a text from memory and preached his sermon, it was a simple, almost pathetic evangelistic effort with every story, every nuance, given exaggerated emphasis and rendered with an attractive accent. Angel was all over the dais, using his body to fullest advantage in conveying the message. When he gave the invitation, there were several responses. People left the church laughing and saying, "Don't let me forget the one about the social worker and the pimp."

Later, my pastor asked what I had thought of Angel's performance. I said I thought that was what it was, a performance, and that I was taken aback by some of his humor.

"He was just softening up the audience," said my pastor. "Don't you like to soften folks up before you try to preach to them?"

Softening up the audience.

But what if God was the audience?

I shudder to think.

Sixth Wrong Teaching

Spiritual People Don't Drink, Dance, or Come Out of the Closet

I can hardly describe the ecstasy I felt when I first learned that Martin Luther, the most important figure in the Protestant Revolution of the early sixteenth century, swore like a drunken sailor. He used the German equivalents of all our four-letter words, and then some. Such speech he classified as among the *adiaphora* — marginal things that have nothing to do with the truly spiritual life. My delight in this discovery, I am certain, stemmed from my sense of revolt against the fussy restrictions of my conservative upbringing.

I myself never liked profanity and rarely employ it except for literary emphasis or in representing somebody else's speech. My father was addicted to bad language, perhaps because he was frustrated in life, and used it constantly in our home. Years later, reading Dostoevsky's *The Brothers Karamazov*, I readily identified with Alyosha, who could not bear to hear his father bellowing out Russian curses and put his hands over his ears to try to shut them out. I still can't bear the casual obscenities in many modern movies and TV programs.

But I delighted in Luther's having been a vile-mouthed religious figure because it somehow vindicated my feeling that there was always something wrong with the conservative and fundamentalist way of identifying spirituality with proper demeanor, and lostness or damnation with cursing, booze, drugs, and illicit sex.

There were many hypocrisies, of course. Drugs were little known in the community of my youth. But my pastor took an obvious delight in slightly off-color stories — not as bad, admittedly, as Angel Martinez's stories — and I could name half a dozen deacons of the church who couldn't stay away from the bottle. One of the leading ministers of our denomination tried to grope my wife at a religious camp when she was fifteen and serving as camp pianist for the week. We heard only recently that a few years later he had to leave his church very suddenly because of an affair with a woman in his congregation that had become public despite all his best efforts to keep it private.

Smoking was generally considered wrong for ministers but all right for the rest of the congregation. I admired our pastor because he walked down Main Street smoking the big cigars he loved, refusing to confine the pleasure to the secrecy of his home. But people gossiped about him terribly, and he died an early death, not only from the effects of smoking, but because there was so much pressure in the congregation for him to resign that he developed lethally high blood pressure.

William Self, a Baptist minister in Atlanta, once said that if he were lost in the city on Sunday morning and needed to find his church, he would just follow the plume of smoke rising heavenward from all the deacons of the church who stood outside to smoke before going in to have prayer and participate in the service.

When I was pastor of the Poplar Grove Baptist Church in rural Rockcastle County, Kentucky, the people told me they could remember the old days when their pastors were actually paid in tobacco and hard liquor. All the members of the church were farmers, whose primary crops were corn and tobacco. They sent the corn to the distilleries on the Kentucky River and received barrels of liquor in return, and they kept some twists of tobacco before transporting the rest to the Lexington markets in November. Some people could recall the old brush-arbor meetings where the little church now stood, when people brought their buggies and wagons and stayed for several days at a time. If word got out that they were having a good meeting, more than a dozen preachers would show up, coming on horseback from as far as fifty or sixty miles away, and they would preach one after another, hour after hour, all day and into the night. When the one who was to preach next noted that the present preacher was weakening, he would go out to his horse, take a bottle from his saddlebag, and get himself liquored-up and into the spirit so he'd be ready to take over.

But after the influence of Carrie Nation and the Women's Christian Temperance Union swept through America, strong drink began to be identified with the devil, and conservative Christianity found it a useful target for invective. Billy Sunday, the famous evangelist, thrilled crowds by tearing into Demon Rum, saying he would fight it as long as he still had teeth in his mouth, and when he no longer had teeth, he would gum it to death.

Our county, like most of the counties in Kentucky where Baptists had a strong hold, voted dry in every election, and this made it hard for most folks to get liquor. They had to know a moonshiner or bring their whiskey in from one of the few wet counties in the state. I worked as a caddy when I was twelve years old, and I used to see one of the local politicians who often went to Frankfort, the state capital, which was wet, come into the clubhouse parking lot with his big automobile nearly dragging the ground in the back. Then I would hear him say to this or that friend, "I've got what you wanted out in the car." After eighteen holes of golf, they would retire to the parking lot, where he sorted out the booze and collected his money, and when he left, the car was riding normally again. I saw many a deacon from

First Baptist Church clutching a paper sack that he carried gingerly to his own car and hid in the trunk.

People in the conservative congregations seemed to like for their ministers to be fierce in their denunciations of drink. It made them feel secure or something. When I was a freshman at Baylor University, I heard R. G. Lee, the widely known minister of Bellevue Baptist Church in Memphis, reputedly the largest church in the Southern Baptist Convention, preach for an hour and forty-five minutes against liquor. His sermon outline was the alphabet. "Booze is *awful*," he began, and spoke for several minutes about how terrible it is. "Booze is *bad*," he said next, and continued his tirade. "Booze is *catastrophic*." And so on he went, cheating when he finally got to *x* by saying, "Booze is *extremely demonic*," or something like that. It was a horrible display of old rhetoric, clichéd conservatism, and wasted time. Afterward I heard several students quip that the sermon was so long and so bad that it was going to drive them to drink!

Years later, when I was academic dean of a small liberal arts college in Louisville, Kentucky, we employed a part-time German professor who had once been pastor of a large Baptist church, where he had enjoyed a growing reputation as a pulpit orator. Then he accepted an invitation to become professor of theology at the Baptist seminary in Rüschlikon, Switzerland, a small institution serving Baptist ministers from all over Europe. He and his wife loved Switzerland, but they were forced to return to the States because his wife had a health problem. He was happy to find work teaching German while his wife's medical needs were being attended and he decided what to do next.

I asked this man one day whether he expected to return to a pastorate. He shook his head slowly and said he wasn't sure he was ready for that. I asked why. He explained that he had spent four years in his last pastorate campaigning to keep organized liquor sales out of his town and county. It had been a terrific conflict, and his family had even endured crosses burned on their lawn. Then he had gone to Switzerland. A few weeks before classes began, he traveled to Basle to sit in on a seminar being given by the eminent theologian Karl Barth. Amazingly, the seminar was conducted in a pub, and the students sat around drinking beer as they listened to Barth. When the minister returned to Rüschlikon, he and his family went to the Baptist church for worship. There, they were astounded to find that the congregation served real wine in Communion.

"I realized," said the man, "that I had spent the best part of my ministry in my last pastorate fighting tooth and nail for something that was a nonissue in Europe. I haven't really recovered from that, and I'm not sure I'm ready to return to the pastorate."

When we left Louisville, we moved to Nashville, where I taught at Vanderbilt Divinity School. The Baptist Sunday School Board is in Nashville, and we had a number of old friends employed there. Whenever they came to dinner at our house, we offered them wine, which they always accepted with great enthusiasm. In fact, they often asked us to go to the ABC store and purchase wine for them, because they had signed a statement at the board that they would not use alcoholic beverages. "If we were seen going into a liquor store," they said, "we would lose our jobs."

I am sure, when I began my spiritual journey as a young pastor, that I sometimes condemned the practice of drinking alcoholic beverages — although never, I am confident, as the main substance of a message. But it was not long before I realized how completely unrelated to Christianity this issue was, and how right Luther was to flout the smaller social conventions that passed for spiritual morality in his environment. Conservative spirituality, in fact, was not spirituality at all, but legalism, and had little to do with the greater issues of the soul's warfare with evil in the world.

When I was pastor of a small Baptist chapel in New Jersey while teaching and doing graduate work at Princeton Theological Seminary, we had a splendid Christian man in our congregation, G. Wayne McCann, who was overseas manager of Occidental Petroleum Company. An attorney by training, Wayne was well-traveled, urbane, articulate, and one of the gentlest, most thoughtful individuals I have ever known. He was also well versed in the Bible and taught the main adult Sunday school class at our church. As I said, our church was actually a chapel in its formative years on the way to becoming a church. Wayne and his wife, Elinor, were mainstays of the congregation financially, socially, and in every other way, and everybody loved them. When I was leaving the congregation after completing my studies at Princeton, it was making plans for a dedication service that would formally constitute it as a church. This change of status involved the election of deacons. As the nominating committee struggled with the task of preparing a slate of officers, several persons naturally thought of Wayne, and said he was by all odds the most likely candidate. There was only one drawback — Wayne and Elinor served wine in their home. Not to the church members, but to many of the overseas visitors they entertained. The matter was debated.

One evening, a delegation from the committee called on Wayne to inform him that they had discussed the possibility of his serving as a deacon but had ruled him ineligible because he used alcoholic beverages. "We don't want you to misunderstand," they said. "We all like you very much. And to show you how much we think of you, we'd like to invite you to give the prayer of ordination for the deacons."

I have often thought of the irony of that decision, and wondered if any of the committee members noticed it. Wayne was the man they deemed most fit to talk with God about the new deacons, but couldn't be a deacon himself because he served wine in his home.

I CAN'T REMEMBER that the word "spirituality" was ever used very much in my church when I was young. I do recall the pastor's preaching on Galatians 5:16–21, where St. Paul contrasted living in the flesh with living in the Spirit. It is a great passage. "Now the works of the flesh are obvious: fornication, impurity, licentiousness, idolatry, sorcery, enmities, strife, jealousy, anger, quarrels, dissensions, factions, envy, drunkenness, carousing, and things like these. . . . By contrast, the fruit of the Spirit is love, joy, peace, patience, kindness, generosity, faithfulness, gentleness, and self-control." Our pastor loved it because the catalogue gave him an excuse for using all those words as the outline of his sermon — or series of sermons, as I think the case once was. He also liked the long, Latinate words in it. "Licentiousness" was almost as good in his register of important words as "lasciviousness" and "concupiscence." I think they gave him a sense of superiority over the grocers and sales people and shop workers in the congregation, for whom he patiently and frequently spelled out their meanings.

In the context of our conservative situation, even this tremendous text seemed far more negative than positive. The preacher made it resound with the multiple sins of our community — all our own "fornication, impurity, licentiousness, idolatry," and so on — but never really did much to make the alternative life of the Spirit sound half so attractive. In fact, he was apt to emphasize the last quality named about life in the Spirit, "self-control," and extol it as something we should always try to exercise, without seeming to recognize that Paul did not list it as something we should practice in our own determination but as a natural concomitant of being filled with the Spirit of God.

We were always being urged to pray, but only in very specific ways — prayers of surrender, so that we could repent of our sins and amend our behavior, and prayers of petition for the sick and for ministers and missionaries everywhere.

The idea that we could actually become spiritual persons — that we could live so constantly in the presence of God that our spirits would recognize his Spirit in everything around us — never seemed to occur to any of the ministers or teachers of my tradition. We were constantly reminded that Jesus prayed a lot, but it was always done with the lesson that he got what he prayed for, never that he became what Marcus Borg in *Meeting Jesus Again for the First Time* calls a " 'spirit person,' a 'mediator of the sacred,' one of those persons in human history to whom the Spirit was an experiential reality."[17]

If I am perfectly honest, I will admit that I find far more spirituality, or true openness to the presence of the loving and the sacred, in the pages of *New Age* magazine than I ever did in the Sunday school or church services of my conservative past. Spirituality, for conservatives and fundamentalists, is essentially self-righteousness. It is following Jesus because he was a teacher of righteousness and trying to live not only by the Ten Commandments but by the much more difficult rules of the Sermon on the Mount. One tries and tries to live up to the moral requirements of the Bible, and when one fails, as is inevitable, he or she collapses into humility and repentance, so that the walk with Jesus is reconstituted. It is a life of repeated failure and triumph, in which the triumph is always short lived and only partially satisfying.

What is the old joke about the woman who got religion at every revival meeting? Smitten by remorse, she would wail, "Fill me, Lord, fill me!" And after hearing this for the tenth or twelfth year, an old brother in the congregation called out, "Don't do it, Lord, she leaks!"

Of course we leak. Of course we fail and cannot keep the promises we make. But that is part of the genius of moralistic religion. It tantalizes us with the hope of a better existence and urges us to try harder. And when we fail, it slaps us in the face with our guilt and urges us to try again. It is a never-ending cycle, and it gives the church a way of perpetually controlling our existence. It also validates our need for a Savior who died on the cross for our sins. It is evident that we cannot ever merit salvation ourselves, for we consistently fail in our attempts to follow him. Therefore we must keep coming back to seek forgiveness and wearily try again.

True spirituality of the kind Jesus knew transcends this pattern of endless failure. It has to do with finding such delight in the presence of the Wholly Other that we spend more and more time there, until our very beings begin to be transformed by the experience. The pattern of failure is broken or simply evaporates. This is not to say we no longer exhibit weakness or fall into failure, for sometimes we do; we are after all only human, not divine. But it is not like the alcoholic returning to booze. It is more like a runner pulling a muscle and having to pay some attention to it, or a pianist having a bad day at the keyboard and waiting for another day to do better. The lapse is easily mended, and the spirit exerts itself with new energy. This is what Paul meant in Galatians 5 — living in the Spirit of God is indeed new life, which leads to all the positive attributes the apostle listed. The negative catalogue — fornication, impurity, licentiousness, idolatry, and so forth — these are not leeches sucking the life out of the triumphant Christian. They describe one who has not yet discovered real spirituality and what it means to exist in God or Christ.

Conservative or fundamentalist Christianity is like a broken record that replays our sins again and again, and asks for repentance over and over. This is why its worship follows an evangelistic pattern and not a true *leitourgos*, or "work of the people." It has never fully understood victorious spirituality in which Christians move to ever and ever higher levels of care and understanding. Its form of worship must always end in the invitation hymn and the hope that someone will have justified all this replaying of the negative side of things by coming under conviction and making a public profession of sin. It does not understand what James Stewart of Scotland called "cultivating the quiet close," in which worshipers take a few moments to absorb the beauty and grace they have shared before exiting to be ministers of love in the world beyond the church. It has trouble comprehending the positive side of Communion, which is about believers sitting quietly in the presence of the risen Lord and feeding on him and what he has given us across the centuries. Fundamentalism sees only the dark and brooding side, about sin and death and punishment.

IF CONSERVATIVES ARE HUNG UP on one thing in particular, it is sex. Maybe they are right to fear it. It is certainly one of the most potent forces in life — we have to assume God made it that way. The novelist D. H. Lawrence understood this and celebrated it in almost every story he wrote. Even now, forty years after reading it, I remember the opening paragraphs of *The Rainbow* and how they describe the coming of spring on the farm of a family named Brangwen. Everything on the farm — trees, animals, people, even the earth itself — is bursting with life. It can't help it; the force is inside it determining everything. And our culture of total permissiveness has certainly unleashed this force with a vengeance, so that wherever we look, from ads in glossy magazines to the latest movies and TV serials to the shows of some TV evangelists, there is a rawness about the sexuality that still shocks most of us who grew up before 1950.

In spite of its pretensions about purity, however, the conservative mind seems to obsess on sex. When I went to church camps as a boy, we didn't even have mixed bathing. The boys swam at one hour and the girls at another. And dancing was out because it involved males and females touching each other outside of marriage — even "rubbing against one another," as the preachers sometimes luridly described it, like two matchsticks bound to produce a conflagration. Only two or three years before I became a Christian, my home church expelled two sisters for attending a dance. They were summoned before the congregation and shamefully dismissed.

There's a widely circulated joke about why Baptists won't have sex standing up — somebody might think they're dancing!

When homosexuals began coming out into society, conservatives were thrown into a frenzy, for they saw this as sex run amok. Jerry Falwell proudly announced that God had sent the AIDS virus as a curse on homosexuals and didn't think medical doctors should try to alleviate the epidemic. There had been plenty of homosexuals before the sexual revolution — indeed, we knew a number who worked for the Baptist Sunday School Board in Nashville — but they were largely tolerated because they behaved discreetly and pretended to be heterosexual. Some even married and had families in order to avoid suspicion.

One of the most terrible stories emerging from the whole panorama of conservative homophobia was that of Dr. Jimmy Allen, who had been minister of the First Baptist Church of San Antonio, Texas, president of the Southern Baptist Convention, and head of a religious cable TV network in Dallas. In his book *Burden of a Secret,* Allen tells the woeful tale of his son Scott, Scott's wife, Lydia, and their two children, Matthew and Bryan.[18] Lydia and Matthew both became HIV-positive through blood transfusions, and Bryan, born after Lydia's infection, was an AIDS baby who died at the age of nine months. Fearful of letting anybody know his daughter-in-law and grandchildren had AIDS, Allen led them all in a conspiracy of silence for more than seven years.

Eventually several national news programs got the story, and Scott and Lydia were interviewed. Allen refused to go on the programs because he was afraid the interviewers would want to discuss another problem — his difficulties with his son Skip, who was a homosexual.

The worst part of the story, however, is the reaction of the Baptist churches Scott Allen and his family tried to attend. Repeatedly, they went to pastors with the warning that their son Matt had AIDS and asked permission to enroll him in Sunday school so he could receive religious instruction with other children his age. Invariably, the reaction was the same. The pastors would have to talk with their staffs or boards of deacons. The staffs and boards of deacons always said no, they could not afford to have an AIDS child in their church.

If this seems to be a twisted picture of conservative spirituality, it is unfortunately only one case among dozens that might be cited.

I remember a conversation my wife had on the phone one night with a pastor friend in a western state who cried as he told her his son was a homosexual and had AIDS. My wife told him we already knew the son was a homosexual because he had come to our church in Los Angeles to help arrange an AIDS benefit for the homosexual community there. "Does your church know?" my wife asked. "Oh no," he said, horrified at the idea, "we can't possibly tell them. I would have to leave the church if we did."

As far as I can recall, Jesus almost never said anything condemning sexuality. He talked about lust in the sayings that form the Sermon on the Mount, and he told the woman taken in adultery to go her way and not to sin again. That story, which occurs in John 8:1–11, is widely regarded by scholars as being a kind of "floater" — it didn't appear in the earliest copies of the Fourth Gospel, and while it may be an authentic story about Jesus, nobody knows where it really originated.

By contrast, Jesus said an awful lot about greed and materialism. Luke's Gospel is literally filled with it — stories of rich rulers and wealthy landowners, men whose preoccupation with wealth almost inevitably diverts them from their worship of God. And conservative churches almost never pillory the men and women in their congregations who have a fever for acquisition. I can't remember that the pastor of my home church ever said anything that might be construed as a criticism of the wealthier members of the congregation. He reminded us almost every Sunday of the evils of drink and debauchery, but never of the subtle power of money or property to derail us from the spiritual life. He did occasionally touch on the text, "You cannot serve God and mammon," but he was always careful not to point it like a loaded pistol at anyone in the congregation. He might have hit a few folks if he had.

The point is, there was — and is — a tacit moral code among conservative and fundamentalist churches that passes for spirituality, while there is almost never any real emphasis on spirituality itself. What it all amounts to is slapping at gnats and swallowing a lot of camel dung. Fundamentalists constantly berate drunkards and drug addicts and homosexuals and liberals, but they almost never display the least understanding of what a truly spiritual life might look like. Their legalistic and negative faith cannot comprehend the meaning of prayer as meditation or as practicing the presence of God. What would they make, I wonder, of the following passage from Janwillem van de Wetering's *A Glimpse of Nothingness,* which is an account of the Dutchman's time in a Zen monastery?

In the Zendo [the hall where meditation is practiced] I bowed to the Buddha statue on the altar. I bowed to my cushion, turned round and bowed again. That way I expressed respect for the man whose teaching had started this religion, to the seat where "I would gain my insight" and to all beings around me. . . . I sat well and the *koan* [a Zen puzzle to aid in the search for enlightenment] gradually became the center of my concentration. Three periods of twenty-five minutes each passed. The fourth period started. Rupert shouted *"Sanzen"* [direct contact between the Zen master and his disciples] and the first group of disciples left the Zendo. I was part of it, being close to the door. We walked in line, quietly. I slipped on a piece of ice and fell. The fat fellow stopped and stood next to me. I got up and shook my head, I was all right. He began to walk again.

We entered the house and knelt in the sitting room. Upstairs, in the *sanzen*-room, the small handbell of the master called the first disciple. My turn came.

You kneel down.

The master looks at you.

You state your *koan.*

The master keeps looking at you. The silence becomes tangible, you can hear the silence.

Tension mounts, very quickly.

And then, for the first time, you are very close to him. There is no distance.

You say nothing, the master asks nothing. Who or what you are is paper-thin. The veil is torn.

The master smiles.

The silence continues and then he gives you the next *koan.* You have a new question and you are in another world.

For a very short moment.

Later you will know that you have been there.[19]

Shortly after this, van de Wetering has his moment of enlightenment. He describes it as almost a no-moment, after which he doesn't feel much different. But he knows he sees things in a new way. A little later, he writes:

Life is misery, and miraculous beauty. The word "miracle" has been used too often and has lost its value. But we live in miracles. The thrushes in the park, the ducks drifting on the canals, the floating seagulls, but also the car on the highway, the mechanical digger in the polder and the large square apartment blocks. Whoever can take the time and the peace to observe is surprised and feels the void of his own being.[20]

How many conservatives and fundamentalists can ever admit to feeling the void of their own being? It requires a special kind of spirituality for this. It isn't a negative void; on the contrary, it is highly, supremely positive. It is what H. A. Williams, the marvelous English priest, felt when he went into Waterloo Station in London about four one afternoon and had time for a cup of tea before boarding his train. As he sat there in the cafeteria looking around at the crowd of travelers having their tea and cakes, his mind played a trick on him. He thought he was at Emmaus and they were all enjoying Communion. "The tea and buns being consumed by the crowd was the broken bread in the midst of which Christ's presence was revealed; and I had once again the immediate certainty of some ultimate reconciliation in which everybody was caught up because they were all filled and alive with God's homely but surpassing glory."[21] Life is indeed a miracle!

Let me cite one more thing. It is a passage from Frederick Buechner's *The Sacred Journey*. Buechner has asked what it means to hear God speaking in the course of our normal days. Then he begins to catalog the sounds he heard around him at home one hot, hazy summer day. There was the twitter of swallows swooping in and out of the barn eaves. Occasionally, in the distance, a rooster crowed. Two men who were doing some carpentry in another part of the house spoke to each other, but their voices were muffled.

He heard his stomach gurgling, signaling that it was almost lunch time. As he listened to these noises, they became the sounds of his own life speaking to him.

> What does the song of a swallow mean? What is the muffled sound of a hammer trying to tell? And yet as I listened to those sounds, and listened with something more than just my hearing, I was moved by their inexpressible eloquence and suggestiveness, by the sense I had that they were a music rising up out of the mystery of not just my life, but of life itself. In much the same way, that is what I mean by saying that God speaks into or out of the thick of our days.[22]

What, in the course of a Christian's life in conservatism or fundamentalism, prepares him or her to appreciate passages like this? To the true conservative, they must be silly, vapid, empty. They certainly would have seemed so to me as a young minister in a conservative church. Yet now, after years along another path, I find them to be the very stuff of my existence, reflections of my own experiences with God in a world where he shines in nearly every face and in every brook and in every turning of the road. I am not a pantheist; I do not think any of these things are God. But by dint of long looking and much praying, I now see him almost everywhere I look — even in the unlikely beginnings of such a journey as mine has been, back there in a fundamentalist church.

Seventh Wrong Teaching

Religion Is a Man's Business

No one ever had to say it. We just knew without reinforcement that running the church was a male prerogative. The women had their own organization, they decorated the church at Christmas and Easter, and they did the cooking for the church dinners. But they never spoke up at business meeting or had speaking parts in the worship services. They knew, as well as the men, what St. Paul had written to the church in Corinth: "Let your women keep silence in the church" (1 Corinthians 14:34).

The pastor of every conservative church I knew was a man. So was the minister of music. So were the deacons. So even were the first educational directors at my home church. No, I take that back. The very first, a part-time director, was a woman. Her name was Sue Johnson, and she was a red-headed knockout. I think the pastor gave her the job without consulting anybody. But she wasn't paid very much and didn't last long. There was a lot of talk about her. The first full-time educational director was male, and the church seemed to breathe easier when he arrived. Every successive educational director has been a man, up to the present day.

Although I was not aware of it at the time, I did know a gifted, attractive young woman in my home church who felt that God was calling her to ministry but was told by our pastor that it was her imagination she was listening to, not the voice of God. She argued with him about this, and also argued with her father, who was a physician and a sort of lay-preacher himself, but to no avail. The door was closed, firmly and irrevocably. After a period of despair, she became active in the statewide work of Baptist women and devoted much of her life to that venue for her considerable talents.

I have met women ministers in United Methodist and Congregational churches who told me they felt called to ministry while they were in conservative churches, but that the ministers of those churches told them to think again, since God couldn't possibly have called them into ministry. W. A. Criswell, longtime minister of the First Baptist Church in Dallas, Texas, publicly stated that any women who believe God is calling them to ministry are flatly mistaken. The ministry in conservative churches is a male preserve, plain and simple. It is like the old men's clubs in Victorian London that were scandalized if a woman even appeared on the premises.

Men in conservative churches are also supposed to be the heads of their households, though everybody knows there are some men who could never be head of any woman, much less the fiercer of their sex. Even as an adolescent, I could tell in church business sessions which men stood to speak because they were being prompted by their wives. I remember one couple in particular. I'll call them Bill and Martha. Bill was a slight little man who clerked in a local bank. His wife was a big, chesty woman with a cheerful face and an outgoing personality. They sometimes sang duets in the worship services, and were really quite good. I imagined as I watched them that he had laced her corset for her, and pictured him bracing his foot against her backside as he pulled at the laces. If the corset straps had ever let loose on a high note, she would have blown them both to Kingdom Come, and the organist with them. No one ever had any doubt about which of them controlled the household. He was meek as a washcloth, and she was dominant as a two-thousand-pound gorilla. And whenever Bill stood in a business meeting to make a comment or a motion, everyone knew it was Martha's idea, and she had drilled him thoroughly in what he must say.

The national Promise Keepers organization that has been in the news a lot in recent years was founded, in part, to remind the male church members of America that they are supposed to be in charge of their households. There is a lot of emphasis on being good partners, too, encouraging loving responsibility for wives and children. But in an age of broken homes, female insurgence, and sexual warfare, Promise Keepers has held a lot of highly publicized pep rallies for men to remind them that the Bible, that literal, inerrant old book, says they are to be the heads of their households and superior to their wives, and that if they want to be fulfilling the will of the Lord they had better get cracking and take back the reins of power in their homes.

Fundamentalist Charlene Kaemmerling says that for women to be in charge of households is "open rebellion against God's design for women."[23] And Bailey Smith, one of the presidents of the Southern Baptist Convention, has gone on record as saying, "I believe the highest calling possible for a Christian woman is to marry a good Christian man, have his children, help him build a Christian home, and hear God speak to her through her husband."[24]

Mrs. Paige Patterson, wife of the president of Southeastern Baptist Theological Seminary in Wake Forest, North Carolina, has been making an effort in recent years to restore male dominance from the distaff side. Her husband is one of the architects of the fundamentalist takeover of the Southern Baptist Convention that occurred over the last two decades, and she has played her part by trying to restore a biblical sense of male-female relationships to the SBC. Whenever she appears in public, even in church, she always wears a hat as a sign of subservience to her husband, reminding people that St. Paul insisted a woman should always have her head covered outside the home. Now she teaches a course at the seminary each semester for the wives of students — there are no female seminarians — to instruct them in how to support their husbands' ministries and to show proper respect for the superiority of the men God has appointed to be their masters.

For those who watch denominational politics, there was an interesting conflict between the new power structure of the Southern Baptist Convention and its distinguished old women's organization, the Women's Missionary Union, headed by a former missionary and educator, Dr. Dellanna O'Brien. The WMU had been founded outside the normal structures of the SBC precisely because it was a woman's organization and was not welcome within the fold. With a chapter in each local church, it had patiently striven across the decades to encourage women to pray for the denomination's mission work and to contribute to its support. Its annual offerings for missionaries had become enormous, and its own organization, including a field of publications, had grown to an incredible size.

When the new order seized control of the denomination, it ordered the WMU to restructure itself within the SBC and surrender control of its sizeable budget. Dr. O'Brien and her cohorts refused. Frantic maneuvering ensued, and the officers of the WMU campaigned vigorously for ongoing control of their own organization. In the end, the women, with their headquarters in Birmingham, Alabama, defeated the new leaders of the SBC in Nashville, and they still manage their own affairs.

In a small way, it was a victory for feminism within the ranks of one of the most male-dominated denominations in America. But it has not diminished the insistence of the new leaders that God intended for women to play second fiddle to men, just as the Bible commanded.

To this day, Southern Baptist churches that dare to install women even as deacons of their congregations face ostracism and expulsion from their sister churches in the area, which form what Baptists call "the Association." A progressive church in the city of Mobile elected a woman to their diaconate. Shortly afterward the church received some new members who began immediately to stir up discord in the rest of the membership. The pastor learned that fundamentalist Baptists in the association had appointed these members to infiltrate his church with the sole purpose of wreaking havoc and forcing him to leave. "It is a common practice," he said. "It happens in many places. They've adopted military tactics to punish churches that dare to elect women to major offices of any kind."

Two or three years ago, I spoke in a Baptist church in South Carolina where a woman had been added to the ministerial staff as director of spiritual life in the congregation. I thought, "What a wonderful thing this church has done! They have not only affirmed a woman in ministry, but have recognized the need for intentional spiritual growth in their membership!" Six months later, I heard from the woman that there was a lot of turmoil in the congregation over her presence and over the senior minister's having selected a woman as a staff member. A short time after that, the senior minister and his entire staff were asked to leave the church. And once more I heard the word "infiltration" — members from fundamentalist churches in the area had invaded the original membership of the church in order to punish those responsible for such openness to women.

THE FEMINIST REVOLUTION had not been a problem for me. My mother was a mild-mannered woman, easily dominated by my father, who was physically larger and came from a very male-dominant farm home. But she had grown up working outside with her father, also a farmer, and never liked being only a housewife and mother. When I was ten years old, she opened an office to help people with their tax returns. She was not a trained accountant, but she had always been very good in math, and she enjoyed the chance to meet people and earn some money of her own. Two or three years later, she became the first female agent in Kentucky for State Farm Mutual Insurance Company, and soon developed a thriving agency.

When the district manager of State Farm needed a good place to employ his son, he peremptorily fired my mother and gave her agency to his son. The son did so poorly, though, and the agency declined so precipitously, that the son had to be let go a couple of years later. The president of State Farm himself drove down from headquarters in Bloomington, Illinois, and begged my mother to take the agency back. She and my father discussed it and decided to take the agency in both their names. The district office would not dare to seize it from my father without just cause. So until their seventies my parents were State Farm agents in our home town, and my mother, who was much more competent than my father, did most of the work in reestablishing a prosperous agency.

By the same token, I had come, through the years of our marriage, to have unbounded respect for the intelligence and abilities of my wife. A woman with a quick, tenacious mind, she had become an astute and indispensable partner to me. Lively and attractive, she was easily the life of any party. Tender and loving, she was a faultless mother to our children. Artistic and hardworking, she kept a beautiful home. Gifted in cookery, she prepared delightful meals. She was also a talented musician, teaching piano in a college and filling our house with the sounds of Mozart and Chopin, Gershwin and Lloyd-Webber. Sometimes she wrote music, and we collaborated on hymns and anthems and full-length musicals. Marriage to her has always been wonderful and fulfilling, and she has taught me, without ever saying it, to hold women in enormous esteem.

I was quite prepared, therefore, when the "women's lib" movement brought an influx of female students to Vanderbilt Divinity School, to find them clever, capable, and entirely worthy of Christian ministry. Almost from the first, they appeared to me superior to most of the male students. They were quicker and more insightful, and their feminine perspective on everything from theology to practical ministry was refreshing and exciting. In my classes on preaching, they brought intimacy and imagination to biblical texts that males had been treating in the same old ways for as long as I had heard men preaching on them. They had a knack for seeing the more caring aspects of a pericope and for developing it with warmth and sensitivity.

One of my students in the early seventies was Ann Denham, the wife of a schoolteacher taking advanced work at George Peabody College for Teachers, across the street from the Vanderbilt campus. Ann was in her thirties then, and mother of several children, but she felt a stirring in her heart to become a minister in the United Methodist Church. Soft and feminine, but with a keen mind and an ability to argue, she could take the measure of any male in her classes.

I vividly remember a sermon she wrote called "Care and the Uppity Woman." It was a Mother's Day sermon during the war in Vietnam, and it emphasized the importance of Christian caretaking in the world. If President Nixon, she said, had had to raise his daughters — had nursed them and got up in the night to care for them when they were sick and held their hands when they were having problems at school — he would have sympathized with all the mothers whose sons were in Vietnam and brought them home. The people who do the caretaking for society, she argued, should be the ones who run society — then we would all live in a saner, more equitable world.

Another woman I recall from those days was Marianna Frost, whose husband, Ken, had been a Dallas Cowboy.

When Ken retired, they bought a dairy farm in southern Tennessee. After Marianna decided to come to seminary and study for the ministry, she got up every morning at five o'clock, helped with the feeding and milking, prepared breakfast, got her family off to work and school, helped with other chores, and drove eighty miles to Nashville for her classes. I remember the journal she wrote for our class in prayer and meditation. She described getting up half an hour earlier to pray before beginning this arduous schedule and how cold the room was as she knelt at her bedside. That was in February. Then, near Easter, she made an entry in which she said, "Just made a great discovery! The time I spend on my knees each morning is preparation for prayer, and then my day becomes the prayer."

There was a young woman who came to divinity school at Samford University while I was there — I'll call her Mindy — who paid a great price to be there. She and her husband had gone as Church of Christ missionaries to Africa or the Middle East and had returned to the States for him to acquire more education. She worked at the university, and in that environment she felt a growing conviction that she should enhance her own education and go into ministry. The Church of Christ in the South — the one that came out of the Christian Church founded by Alexander Campbell in the mid-nineteenth century — is extremely fundamentalist. It is so insistent on the literal interpretation of Scripture that it refuses to practice anything it doesn't find endorsed by the New Testament. As it cannot point to a New Testament religious service in which musical instruments were employed, it does not allow musical accompaniment in its churches. Mindy's husband, less liberated than she, opposed her becoming a minister. When they couldn't reach an accommodation, she decided she had to leave him and follow her heart. She was an excellent student, and I have no doubt she is serving some denomination now as a fine pastor.

All over the U.S., women are pouring into mainstream seminaries. Many of them are from conservative and even fundamentalist backgrounds — Southern Baptists, Pentecostalists, Nazarenes, Assemblies of God — and know there won't be a place to serve in their denominations when they complete their education. They only know God is calling them to ministry and figure he will show them the way when they arrive at the point where they need to know. And the conservative churches will be the poorer for losing them. They ridicule and shut out women who assert their right to enter a ministry long dominated by men, but history will show them to be narrow-minded and shortsighted. Eventually even the Roman Catholic Church will ordain female priests. It is only a matter of time and maturation.

OF COURSE THE BIBLE doesn't promote the forwardness of women in religious matters. It is itself the product of a male-dominated society in an era when women were regarded as chattel and had almost no rights. But a person has to be terribly obtuse not to see what an important part women played in the birth of Christianity. It is obvious from a number of references in the Gospels that a band of women as well as men followed Jesus. Luke's Gospel even says that some wealthy women financed the itineracy of Christ and his other followers (Luke 8:3). Even in a world where women's names were seldom mentioned in writing, we know the names of several women dear to Jesus. And it was to the women, not the men, that the Resurrection was first revealed.

It is also clear from the Book of Acts and the letters of Paul that women formed a mainstay of the early church, often opening their homes to little bands of believers for their meetings. In an age when life was highly uncertain and people often died young, there were many widows who inherited their husbands' estates and made them available to the fledgling church. In several of Paul's epistles there are special greetings to the women who had been invaluable to him in the organizing and establishing of churches.

To refuse women the right to ordination and service in the church in any age is therefore highly unthinkable, especially in contemporary society, which, enlightened about gender roles, offers women the same opportunities as men to become doctors, lawyers, teachers, military personnel, and CEOs.

It is amusing, according to Dr. Joel Gregory, who spent two years as W. A. Criswell's associate at First Baptist Church, Dallas, in the expectation of succeeding him as senior minister, to know how Criswell handled the matter of his wife's teaching a large Sunday school class — between two and three hundred people — each Sunday in their church. Criswell often went on record saying that no woman ought ever to have authority over a man, even in the classroom. But in the case of his wife's class, he said it was all right because *he* delegated the authority to her to be a teacher of both men and women.

And even Jerry Falwell has managed to host Roman Catholic fundamentalist Phyllis Schlafly as "speaker" at the "main preaching service" at Thomas Road Baptist Church by putting his imprimatur on her appearance and denying that she was actually preaching to the congregation:

> Being a Baptist, we've never had a woman preacher here. We Baptists don't ordain women. But may I say to you, that if I ever ordained a woman and if she ever requested it — and I won't, I promise — it would be Mrs. Phyllis Schlafly. . . . You'll be hearing from Phyllis in just a few moments. She is not going to *preach,* she's going to *talk.* Don't get nervous, Baptists. She's going to *talk.*[25]

In 1991, I was chair of a faculty committee at Samford University to stage a sesquicentennial celebration of Christianity and the arts. As the date for the celebration drew near, we were having trouble locating an attractive speaker to provide the opening address. We had asked one prominent Christian novelist, but he did not respond to phone calls and letters. I telephoned our friend Madeleine L'Engle to do the honors, but learned she was in Antarctica or some exotic location giving lectures for the U.S. State Department. About that time, CBS *Sunday Morning* showed an interview with General Norman Schwarzkopf in the Far East. The interviewer asked if the Gulf War wasn't terribly stressful to him. The general said yes, but every night he read from a book called *Joshua* by a former Roman Catholic priest named Joseph Girzone. Joshua, we were informed, was a modern Christ figure living in a small town in New York State. Then the show broadcast an interview with Father Girzone. Smitten by his winsome appearance, I went out and bought a copy of *Joshua* and read it.

I got Father Girzone's number from directory assistance and invited him to our celebration. As luck would have it, he had a trip planned to Mississippi a few days before our conference and said he would be glad to swing by Birmingham on his way back.

Samford University had never had a Roman Catholic to speak in its chapel, and I was frankly concerned about whether he would be welcome in this Baptist university. So I invited Father Girzone to stay in our home. His address was so successful that he overwhelmed our faculty, students, and visitors with his ingenuous message about Jesus. We had a hard time getting people out of the auditorium after his talk to make room for the next event — and he, my wife, and I struck up a wonderful friendship in our home. Before he left, I asked Joe — no more "Father Girzone" stuff — to come back, stay with us a few months, and write a novel about Joshua in the South. I assured him he would find plenty of religious controversy there to fill a book. Joe's

reply was, "I don't like grits." Then he unpacked his statement — he was a Northerner and didn't really understand
the Southern milieu well enough. "Why don't you do it?" he
threw at me.

It was an attractive idea, but I couldn't use Joe's character.
He is such a gracious man that I am sure he would have
agreed to my doing so, but I simply couldn't bring myself
to employ Joshua in a fictional work of my own. So I tried
to dismiss the idea. But it kept coming back. What could
I do? Finally I had the idea of making the contemporary
Jesus character a woman and calling her Jessie. Jessie was my
mother's name, and it was as close to "Jesus" as I could get.

Jessie: A Novel was published by McCracken Press in
1993. McCracken Press was a new enterprise for Jarrell
McCracken, the great Texan who had founded Word Books
four decades earlier. Unfortunately, this promising press
soon faltered and failed within a couple of years of its inception, so not many people ever heard of *Jessie*. Some who did,
however, said it was one of the most liberating books they
had ever read, because it raised a lot of questions about our
old gender distinctions in the Christian religion.

I made Jessie an artist who migrated from New Haven,
Connecticut, to the area around Gatlinburg, Tennessee.
There she felt God leading her to paint a series of portraits
of "Great Women in Religion" — several biblical women,
some medieval saints, and a few modern figures, including
Mother Teresa and Rosa Parks, the determined African-
American woman who refused to move to the back of a
bus in Montgomery. As the paintings emerged, people took
sides for and against them — and the leading fundamentalist preachers of the area took Jessie to task as an emissary
of Satan and an enemy of organized religion. Like Jesus,
she died a horrible death at the hands of hired assassins,
but then miraculously appeared again to a large number of
followers.

I feel confident that one day *Jessie* will be rediscovered and will speak to a lot of people about the issue of women and ministry. What it proclaims, I believe, is the likely possibility that if Christ had come not in the time of patriarchy, but our own time, God's messenger would have been a woman. Messiahship has nothing to do with gender. That was an accident of time and place. God has always worked through women as well as men, and will do so even more, now that society has caught up to the divine understanding of female worth.

Consider, for example, this information released in 2000 by the Barna Research Group of California: Nearly 60 percent of all U.S. Christians are women; only 40 percent are men. By their own estimate, 79 percent of the women who are Christians consider themselves "spiritual," while only 63 percent of the male Christians would lay claim to such characterization. Of these, 69 percent of women say they are "very spiritual," while only 50 percent of the men adjudge themselves similarly. Twice as many women as men are involved in some form of active Christian discipleship. Among all Christians volunteering for service of any kind, there are 33 percent more women than men. Among those who read the Bible regularly, 29 percent more are women. Among those who pray daily, 16 percent more are women. Women are clearly more involved in American Christianity than men.

At the turn of the millennium, only 5 percent of U.S. churches are headed by a female pastor. But that is a significant increase over a century ago. And while conservative and fundamentalist churches will doubtless hold out against the ordination of women for a long time to come, it is an easy prediction that the number of churches with women ministers will soon double and even triple because of the growing fashion in the moderate and liberal churches. God doesn't have a problem with female ministers — it is only some religious groups who do!

THERE WAS DELICIOUS IRONY in something that transpired a few years ago at Southern Baptist Theological Seminary in Louisville. It was after the advent of President Al Mohler, who was sent in by the fundamentalists wanting to get rid of a professor named Molly Marshall and any women intending to become ministers. The preaching department of the seminary announced its annual sermon contest for all the students. Participants were to submit sermon manuscripts without putting names on them. Their names were registered separately on a numbered list, and their numbers alone appeared on the manuscripts, so that the judges of the contest could not possibly play favorites.

When the judging was over and the top three sermons selected, the person in charge of organizing the contest consulted the list to match the winning numbers to the names of the students. Imagine his surprise when he found that all of the top three preachers were women!

That should have told the administration and faculty something. But it didn't. Some moderate and liberal denominations are going to get some great preachers.

Eighth Wrong Teaching

Faith Is Always Truer Than Science

God created the world and the heavens in only six days (Genesis 1–2:3). When Moses threw his staff on the ground, it became a snake; when he picked it up, it became a staff again (Exodus 4:1–5). God sent plagues of blood, frogs, boils, and other things on the Egyptians (Exodus 7–12). When Moses stretched his hand over the Red Sea, God parted the waters and the Israelites walked through on dry land (Exodus 14:21–22). The prophet Elisha made an ax head float in the water (2 Kings 6:5). Joshua ordered the sun to stand still while God gave a great victory to the Israelites over the Amorites, and it lingered in the heavens a whole day without setting (Joshua 10:12–14). Elijah rode to heaven in a chariot of fire (2 Kings 2:11). When a widow needed money to save herself and her sons from slavery, the prophet commanded her to fill more vessels from her container of oil, and every time she poured some oil, the original vessel was refilled (2 Kings 4:1–7). When Daniel was shut up in the lions' den, God sent an angel that stopped the mouths of the lions so they could not harm him (Daniel 6:22). Jonah was swallowed by a great fish, remained in its belly for three days and nights, and at God's command was spewed out on dry land (Jonah 1:17–2:10). At the command of Jesus, his friend Lazarus, who had been dead four days, arose and came out of his tomb (John 11:43–44). Ananias and Sapphira were struck dead by God for withholding money from the early Christian community (Acts 5:1–11). An angel appeared to

Simon Peter, struck off his wrist chains, and delivered him from prison (Acts 12:6–11).

The Bible is packed with incredible material, and conservatives insist that we believe every word of it.

I did, when I was a young man. I was like the queen in *Alice in Wonderland,* who set herself to believing six things that weren't true every morning before breakfast. I was told faith had to believe it. If I wavered on anything the Bible said, I was in danger of hellfire.

It wasn't really hard. I was a romantic, so I saw nothing wrong with insisting that the Bible was true even if it made the whole world false. I hadn't yet heard of *Credo quia absurdum est,* but I understood the principle and was willing to stand on it. I thought I was being a true follower, siding with God against a faithless world. I didn't care who laughed or misunderstood. After all, faith was clearly superior to reason and science.

I was fairly adept at science courses in school, and I did well in math and enjoyed puzzles of any kind. One of my physics professors in college, a warm and delightful man named H. Y. Mullikin, even confided to a friend, who in turn told me, "The world lost a great scientist when God called John Killinger into the ministry." That dear man greatly overestimated my ability. But I simply had no interest in being a scientist. Religion was the only thing I cared about — religion and the arts, because I found the arts so expressive of religious thoughts and feelings.

I can recall precisely where I was when I had my first serious doubt about the conservative attitude toward the truths of scientific investigation. I was then in graduate school at the University of Kentucky, studying literature and philosophy, and I was walking along a sidewalk on South Limestone Street bound for our little apartment on Waller Avenue. I had been reading the novels of Theodore Dreiser, the author of *Sister Carrie* and *An American Tragedy* and a number of other important texts of early twentieth-century American realism, and I was thinking about Dreiser and the events in his life that had made him antireligious. He was the son of Midwestern street evangelists and grew up hating their humiliating lifestyle and refusal to discuss the possibility that Darwin was right about the natural world's having evolved from simpler beginnings.

One day when he was a boy, young Dreiser had gone with his mother to the grocery store where she shopped. The grocer had a fish tank in front of the store, and had placed a lobster and a squid in it. The lobster tried to catch the squid, but each time the squid would emit an inky substance and escape from the lobster's grasp. Dreiser was fascinated and continued to go back to the store every day to see what was happening in the tank. Eventually the squid began to weaken. It did not produce as much of the inky liquid as before and could not dart away with the same swiftness. One day the lobster managed to catch a piece of the squid, and the next day another. Finally the squid no longer had the strength to escape, and the lobster finished it off.

The doctrine of survival of the fittest became a cornerstone of Dreiser's thinking, and his novels, influenced partly by the French realists but expressive of his own strong scientific bias, revealed human beings caught in the inexorable jaws of circumstance, from which only the strongest and cleverest ever managed to extricate themselves. Traditional Christian religion — the kind his parents so abhorrently represented to him — was always powerless against the forces of nature, and his characters were mere pawns in the resolution of conflicting forces beyond their own line of vision.

That day as I walked along between the university and our apartment I felt a chill go through my entire body as a single question sounded in my brain: "What if Dreiser is right, and the world is controlled not by God but by the interplay of certain inevitable forces already at work in time and history? Suppose the Bible is only the record of certain primitive minds trying to cope with their human situations, and its understanding is simply erroneous and not applicable to reality as we can now comprehend it. Have I pledged my life to something built on mere illusion?" It was a frightening question, and one I would face again and again in the course of my life. Once it has occurred, there is never a moment when one is entirely free from it. It casts its long shadow over the whole of one's journey.

I have mentioned earlier that I had a visitation from an angel when I was sixteen years old. That experience anchored my soul through times of turbulence. I am still convinced of the reality of the visitation. I had not been thinking in any way about angels. I was praying at the time, kneeling at my bedside, but I was not sleepy and was fully conscious. The angel's appearance was not what I would have imagined had I been trying to conceive of such a being. I knew, though not a single word was spoken, that it was the angel Gabriel. He stood in the corner of my room, tall, luminous, and commanding. His hands were extremely long, like the hands in an El Greco painting, and his face was gaunt. Probably the visit lasted only a few seconds, but, like other numinous experiences I've read about, it seemed timeless. As I have said, I was actually disappointed, on reflection, that the visitor was not Christ himself. The appearance was so startling, so completely unbidden, that I can picture it as vividly today as I saw it then. It was a real experience, not a hallucination, and I believe it was intended precisely as an anchor to hold my faith steady through repeated exposures to ideas and philosophies that might otherwise have shifted it.

Once I had entertained that first doubt about the absolute truthfulness of the Scriptures — that is, their factual truth in relation to the empirical truth of a scientific worldview — I began to look more critically at the conflict between biblical accounts of what happened in ancient times and the findings of modern science. My thoughts weren't consumed by the conflict, as I was very busy trying to juggle graduate studies and my weekend pastoral duties, but I gradually came to an accommodation between my old literalist views of Scripture and an acceptance of certain scientific facts. It never became important to me to distance myself from biblical statements, either privately or publicly; I was merely content to accept the possibility that the writers of the Bible inhabited a more primitive culture in which fanciful explanations of events were more acceptable than they would be today. Many of the far-fetched descriptions of events given in the Bible, I was certain, accrued to those events over the centuries after they had happened. Somebody along the line gave a fanciful explanation of the Israelites' escape from Egypt or a prophet's recovery of an ax head that had fallen in the river, and it got written into the tribal account. As for the creation of the world, the story in Genesis was undoubtedly a beautiful, mythic response of some father or grandfather to his children when they said, "Grandpa, where did the world come from?" All of these were *forgivable* lapses from everyday truth as long as I didn't take the text too seriously, and didn't impugn the spiritual truth of the Scriptures.

LITTLE WAS MADE, during my youth in the church, of the great evolution controversy that had rocked conservative Christendom in the nineteenth century and was again to shake American education in the 1960s and 1970s. The whole matter had simply gone underground after the Scopes trial in 1925. The outcome of that trial, favorable to the fundamentalists who insisted that local school boards could control what their children were studying in public schools, nevertheless discredited fundamentalist teaching about the origins of the world and its inhabitants. The effect was pretty much like the aftermath of the Civil War, when the Southern states, under President Andrew Johnson, himself a Southerner, simply went back to preemancipation ways in the treatment of the Negro. People didn't talk much about it, but they continued to teach their children that the Bible was literally right, God had created the world in six days, and anybody who said otherwise was a modernist fool.

Mark Noll, in *The Scandal of the Evangelical Mind,* devotes a whole chapter to what he calls "The Intellectual Disaster of Fundamentalism." Fundamentalists, he says, failed to see that William Jennings Bryan lost the debate at Dayton, Tennessee, and continued to shape their worldviews around a "Bible-onlyism" that was blind to the discoveries of science. They clung to a theology that "did not provide Christian guidance for the wider intellectual life," and because of this, "there has been, properly speaking, no fundamentalist philosophy, no fundamentalist history of science, no fundamentalist aesthetics, no fundamentalist history, no fundamentalist novels or poetry, no fundamentalist jurisprudence, no fundamentalist literary criticism, and no fundamentalist sociology. Or at least there has been none that has compelled attention for insights into the way God has made the world and situated human beings on this planet."[26]

I remember the biology class I took in high school. Taught by a maiden lady who was both a churchgoer and a sports enthusiast, its sole focus was on the classifications of plants and animals, together with a smattering of knowledge about how certain animal bodies were constructed. We dissected frogs and grasshoppers and looked at certain tissues through microscopes, always with the kind of ineptness and general hilarity that made me a lifelong fan of humorist Robert Benchley's essay in which he described being able to see nothing in a microscope lens but the reflection of his own eye. There was never a mention of evolution or of the possibility that even the animals we studied more carefully than others had in any way changed to adapt to their surroundings. No student ever left biology class with a question about how things came to be the way they were, or whether there was any conflict at all between modern scientific investigation and traditional religious faith. In fact, there was never a mention of Charles Darwin.

The crisis was only in hiatus, of course, because the fundamentalist preachers were still fuming over the impudence of the Darwinians and the educators who were preparing more responsible textbooks and class aids for use in biology courses in public schools. The centennial in 1959 of the appearance of Darwin's *On the Origin of Species* spurred biology teachers at the National Science Foundation's summer institute to complain that textbooks lagged woefully behind refinements in research in their field. A group of distinguished scientists formed the Biological Sciences Curriculum Study and received seven million dollars from the NSF to pursue work on new materials for the classroom. In 1963, after extensive preparation and testing, the group marketed three introductory textbooks for high school classes, each based on evolutionary assumptions as "the warp and woof of modern biology."

Fundamentalist response was swift and vicious. Many Southern school superintendents refused to buy the books. The Rev. Reuel Lemmons of the Church of Christ, which boasted two-thirds of a million members in Texas alone, appealed to the Texas board of education and to Governor John Connally to ban the books in that state, claiming they were "pure evolution from cover to cover, completely materialistic and completely atheistic." When the state textbook selection committee met in the fall of 1963, they approved the books but insisted that publishers soften the evolutionary language in them, largely nullifying the modernizing effect of the texts.

Conservative and fundamentalist preachers, recognizing a popular whipping boy, began preaching and demonstrating regularly against the godless materials of federal education groups and insisting on a return to traditional values and understanding of God's supreme control over creation. Herbert W. Armstrong, who organized the World Wide Church of God based in California and was a widely known radio and TV preacher, regularly deplored the "missing dimension of moral and spiritual values" in modern education. Carl McIntire, a fundamentalist radio preacher on the East Coast, acquired three hundred acres at Cape Canaveral as a "freedom center" for his Twentieth Century Reform Movement and assailed evolution and other godless scientific teachings of our time. Billy James Hargis, a fundamentalist voice from Arkansas, consistently struck a similar note, insisting that our schools return to the teaching of creationism as a prerequisite for America's recapturing of its earlier greatness. The Jehovah's Witness society's magazine *Awake,* with a distribution of 7.5 million copies, called for its membership to rise up against the teaching of evolution, calling it "the greatest fairytale ever to masquerade under the name of science."

As the fundamentalists went to court in the 1960s and 1970s, their scientifically trained proponents of creationism insisted that the chronology for the creation of the world developed in the seventeenth century by Archbishop James Ussher was correct, and that the exact date of the world's beginning was 4004 B.C. They cited evidence from fossils and rock formations to suggest that the world had been created very suddenly, not over long periods of time, and that the great flood in the time of the biblical character Noah really did occur. God created the world some six thousand to ten thousand years ago, they said; and instead of all life deriving from a single source millions or billions of years ago, God created the "various kinds" of living things with their individual genetic structures. For the most part, they spent their time and energy trying to pick apart evidence for evolution, denying the value of radioisotope dating to determine the ages of existing matter. Creation research societies abounded, usually funded by right-wing religious or political activists, and all over the country parents' groups proliferated that were willing to go to the mat with school boards and educators about what was best for their children. State education boards began softening the language of textbooks, removing an air of dogmatism about evolution. The activists even reached Ronald Reagan, who told reporters during his first electoral campaign that evolution theory had been seriously challenged: "It is not believed in the scientific community to be as infallible as it once was believed. But if it is going to be taught in the schools, then I think that the biblical theory of creation should also be taught."

One of the greatest advantages enjoyed by the creationists was the growing consensus among astrophysicists that the earth was originally created by a "Big Bang," a moment of cataclysmic explosion in the galaxy that produced precisely the right conditions for life to begin on our planet. The scientists also said the evidence is incontrovertible that the development of the various species of life on the planet required millions or billions of years. Therefore the fundamentalists point to these two arguments as contradictory, claiming that they show the ridiculousness of scientific theory and insisting that the traditional view of creation by divine fiat actually makes better sense than the newer, scientific view.

For me personally, the whole controversy from beginning to end — though the end is not in sight — has only underlined the distance my thinking has come from the determined stance of my earliest mentors in the faith. I do not care that the Bible is a book of poetry, not of science, and that it is frequently in error about the manner in which things happened. It is enough for me that those who wrote the Bible understood a lot about life and how it should be lived, without expecting them to be correct about scientific matters. To try to hold faith and science together at the expense of either is pure fatuousness — though I understand that the fundamentalists must do it in order to preserve their doctrine of biblical infallibility.

The awkwardness and stupidity of this position fills me with pain. Why must good people make such asses of themselves in the name of religion? They can see the folly of Muslims who willingly throw away their lives in holy wars they cannot possibly win. They can even see the foolishness in faith healers who refuse medical care for themselves and their children in situations where the afflicted are going to die without basic help. Why can't they see it in their own logically indefensible position?

God doesn't need an inerrant Bible to be God. True believers shouldn't need it either.

As a MINISTER, I never made it my business to go out of my way to trouble parishioners with a more literal approach to the Bible by saying that no intelligent person in the modern world could really accept such a ridiculous account of things. Like Benjamin Franklin, who said he read the Bible the way he ate fish, simply laying aside the parts that might get caught in his throat, I learned to live by the deep wisdom of the Scriptures without worrying about their literal facticity. If I preached on the creation story in Genesis, it was only to speak of the creativity of God or the beauty of the created order, not to apply a calculator and modern timetable to the schedule by which creation occurred.

I readily admit the dilemma such a careless approach puts me into — the one the fundamentalists think they avoid by insisting on an all-or-nothing policy when it comes to reading the Scriptures. It does raise the question of what to do with the miracles of Jesus in the Gospels — especially the raising of Lazarus — and with the matter of the Resurrection, which certainly thumbs its nose at any physical science I have ever known about. How can I attribute the Old Testament stories to exaggeration and hyperbole and not submit the New Testament stories to the same test?

I am not really sure I can answer that question. I feel that I am dealing somehow with different levels of plausibility. My mind recognizes that the Resurrection of Jesus is as far-fetched, from a logical, scientific viewpoint, as the parting of the Red Sea or Jonah's three-day stay in the belly of a great fish. Yet I find the Resurrection much more important to faith than the other stories. It stands so dead center in the whole of Christian mythology — so that the very existence of the early church seems somehow to spring from it — that I cannot dismiss it the way I do the other "tall tales." It is like the black box on an airplane that reports information from the very heart of an otherwise unknowable situation. More than anything else in our tradition, it is the key to something transcendent, the signature of an alternative dimension to human existence.

Why can I believe the Resurrection when I cannot believe that an ax head floated or the sun stood still for twenty-four hours? I can believe it because it is not out of character with the most intense spiritual experiences I have had, such as the visitation of the angel when I was sixteen. And a mystical moment that occurred years later, when I was in my thirties. It was very early, and the dawn was just coming as I drove through the hills of Northern Kentucky on my way from Louisville to Cincinnati. I was on back roads, as I planned to stop by my maternal grandfather's house for breakfast before proceeding to my appointment in Cincinnati. The road wound crookedly through the countryside, hugging the very sharp and knobby hills, and I was driving only twenty or thirty miles an hour. I was rounding a

very tight curve at the precise moment when the rays of the
barely risen sun were caught full force in a cattle pond beside some farmer's barn. The sudden brilliance of the sight
nearly blinded me. The pond appeared to contain the sun as
if it were right there, burning with incredible luminescence,
in a large bowl. I was smitten, astounded, totally entranced.
I felt as if everything in existence had been compressed into
a fiery unity in that pond and I was momentarily at the heart
of all mystery. It couldn't have lasted more than a few seconds, for the car continued to move and was soon past the
barn and the pond. Yet it was an experience out of time
and continued to haunt my thoughts for days and weeks.
Even now, many years later, my heart seizes up slightly when
I think about it.

I believe the Resurrection was an experience of this nature, something in which the apostles saw to the very core
of human existence and realized that it is mystically insep-
arable from God himself. Those other things — the parting
of the sea, the floating ax head, Jonah in the fish, the sun
standing still — are of a lower order of miracle. They are
bragging stories, astonishing tales. But the Resurrection is
different. It is an insight into deepest mystery, into the way
all things cohere in God.

Consider the experience novelist and screenwriter Dan
Wakefield reports in his book *How Do We Know When It's
God?*:

> One night when I am nine years old I go to bed, say the
> Lord's Prayer, and before going to sleep (I feel clearly
> and vividly awake during this whole experience), I feel
> or sense — I *experience* — my whole body filling with
> light. The light is white and so bright that it seems al-
> most silver. It is not accompanied by any voice or sound,
> but I know quite clearly the light is Christ, the pres-
> ence of Jesus Christ. I am not transported anywhere,

I am all the time in my room at the top of the stairs in our house at 6129 Winthrop, Indianapolis, Indiana, a place as familiar as my own hand. Everything is the same as always, my bed and the desk across from it, the pictures on the wall of my favorite football heroes, like Tommy Harmon of Michigan. Everything is normal and solid and real, the only thing different is the Light, and after it has infused me, maybe I too am different, or in some way changed — not better or brighter or nicer but simply changed, the way a person is changed by deep experience, altered in how the world is perceived, more open to the unexplainable, the great mysteries, the gift of grace. The light is not frightening to me as a child, but reassuring, like a blessing. It is so real that in fact it seems today like the very bedrock of my existence.[27]

Somehow, the miraculous, transcendent nature of Christ in the Resurrection is of an order linked to this. To me, it bespeaks something so far beyond ordinary experience as to be almost incredible, yet beckons with a power I cannot deny. The other miraculous things in the Bible — excluding some of the miracles associated with Christ himself — are of insignificance to me. It does not matter whether they occurred as reported in the Bible or not. The transcendence of Christ, on the other hand, is of tremendous importance. It is the one place in all the biblical witness where I can stare into a light and see something beyond it — in fact, where I can see a whole world of supernal existence for which our descriptions of heaven are but a clumsy form of shorthand.

WHILE I WAS WRITING this very page, the telephone rang. It was a friend calling from Michigan to tell me about a strange experience he has just had. A man in his forties, Jim (not his real name) is a fine trumpeteer who played for years with the U.S. Army Band, often traveling with Bob Hope and other celebrity entertainers. His father is a pentecostalist lay minister in Tennessee and has often expressed uneasiness with Jim's life as an itinerant musician. A few days earlier, Jim was in a car accident and a broken rib punctured an artery. He did not realize this until several nights later, when he was stricken with acute pains in his stomach and began coughing up blood. He called a friend to take him to the hospital.

While waiting for the friend to arrive, Jim dialed his father on his cell phone and told him something was frightfully wrong and that he was going into the hospital. His father began to pray for him over the phone. Suddenly, said Jim, his father started speaking in tongues. Then the words became recognizable again. But now it was not his father's voice he was hearing. Instead, it was a much deeper, more penetrating voice. Jim, almost in a coma, knew it was the voice of God speaking to him through his father.

"Jim," the voice said, "you are an extremely talented man, but you have not been living for me as I want you to. You are going to pull through this — I will see to that — but you have got to get your act together and begin serving me with your music."

"I passed out then," said Jim. "When I came to, we were already at the hospital and they were wheeling me into surgery. But I remembered every word I had heard, and I wasn't afraid. When I went home, several days later, the first thing I did was call my dad. I hadn't been able to call him in the hospital because I didn't have my credit cards with me. I said, 'Dad, do you remember what you said to me as I was on the way to the hospital?' He said, 'No, son, I'm afraid I don't. I wasn't conscious of anything I was saying. I was only the transmitter.'"

Jim was profoundly affected by this experience. Unless I am wrong, it will be a pivot on which his whole life changes.

He certainly sounded deeply impressed when he called me this afternoon.

Now, what am I to make of this report? Was Jim hallucinating? Did he hear a voice his subconscious needed to hear? Or was there something divine, something truly supernatural, in what he experienced? I am frankly inclined to the latter answer, for it is of the same broad nature to me as the Resurrection of Jesus and other extraordinary experiences I have encountered or heard about across the years.

PHYSICISTS AND MATHEMATICIANS from Einstein to Hawking have been trying to tell us that the world isn't constructed exactly as we had thought it was, that the simple Newtonian physics we learned in high school and college may adequately explain certain phenomena of a limited sort, but something far deeper and more all-embracing is required to account for the behavior of everything in the multiverse, in which our planet is a mere speck whirling amid countless stars and planets much larger and more important to the patterned stability of all that exists. Their discoveries have already established connections between science and religion that fifty years ago none of us ever believed would be there, and have pointed us to the hope that one of these days, when our knowledge of the universe is several times greater than it is today, God or something very like God will turn out to be the mysterious "unifying theory" everybody is now seeking to explain how things are related and work as they do.

John Updike has phrased it this way through the mouth of Dale Kohler, a character in *Roger's Version:*

> The most miraculous thing is happening.... The physicists are getting down to the nitty-gritty, they've really just about pared things down to the ultimate details, and the last thing they ever expected to happen is hap-

pening. God is showing through. They hate it, but they can't do anything about it. Facts are facts. And I don't think people in the religion business, so to speak, are really aware of this — aware, that is, that their case, far-out as it's always seemed, at last is being proven.[28]

The important thing the new physicists have seen and reported is that matter and energy do not have a fixed, particular existence — everything that exists is in motion, is part of the divine dance of the galaxies, and is accountable only to higher regulations whose roots we have not yet discovered. It may have seemed incredible, even impossible, that Jesus should appear to his disciples in the upper room after the Resurrection even though they had bolted the door against intruders. But suppose death involves transcending the ordinary barriers to such behavior, so that like the atoms themselves we move in and through what appear to be physical obstructions.

Imagine a field full of fireflies on a summer night. They are flying this way and that, up and down, in and out among all the others, and they leave little trails of light everywhere they go. Soon the night sky is an etching of their lighted trails. But they themselves grow dark and disappear, leaving behind the lighted etching. Amazed, you approach the light and reach out your hand. There is something there. Your hand brushes reality when it sweeps through the air. It isn't only a vision, it is actual. According to the "uncertainty principle" of quantum mechanics, the elementary particles of matter only *seem* to be in particular places, but are not there when physicists look for them. Yet the evidence of their having been there remains and is real.

Sound spooky? Yes. But aren't we right in saying that modern science is becoming more spiritual, that it is verging toward explanations of the supernatural as well as the natural? Maybe the Resurrection of Jesus and all those appearances he made to the disciples were not as far-fetched as we thought, but in fact were glimpses into this spirit-world transcending the world where we *think* we are presently living. And the reports of people who have had near-death or life-after-life experiences may be further glimpses, peeks through the keyhole of eternity into a manner of existence we are not yet prepared to understand.

This is why I differentiate between the miraculous aura around Jesus Christ and the tall tales of the Old Testament — also some of the tall tales in Acts. The tall tales are gratuitous, mere excrescences of the human imagination. But Jesus and everything associated with him may provide a clue to something beyond the human imagination, something we are yet to discover even though it was in our past.

A few years ago, when I was in Paris writing a book on the theater of the absurd, I went on a lovely Sunday afternoon in April to the tiny Théâtre du Rochechouart, in the back streets of the city, to see a play by Fernando Arrabal called *Le Cimétière des voitures (The Car Cemetery)*. It was a small theater, and we entered by a ramp that actually crossed part of the stage, which was built around all four walls of the room, and we sat in rotating chairs in the center. The play, which is absolutely nonsensical, without plot or characterization, consisted of two hours' worth of shouting, posturing, and physical pursuit around the perimeter of the room, with the players constantly banging on old cars with ball bats or swinging heavy chains against sheets of metal hanging from the rafters. What's more, the lights — powerful klieg lights — were randomly rotated, so that they struck the audience in the eyes as much as they focused on the stage. Within minutes, I thought I would have to leave the theater or go mad. But I couldn't get out; the ramps had been withdrawn when the doors were closed. I would have to make the best of it.

Eventually, maybe in fifteen or twenty minutes, I began to relax, swing around in my chair, and accept the antics of the actors as natural and worth watching. And two hours later, when the play was over, the ramps were replaced, and the doors were opened, I staggered out into the quiet street, where I heard some children playing and the distant barking of a dog. The silky leaves on the trees reminded me that spring had arrived. I stood there, frozen by what I was seeing and hearing. It seemed vastly less real than what I had seen and heard inside. I wanted to turn and go back into the theater, back to the kind of reality to which I had so quickly become accustomed there.

This experience was one of the greatest lessons of my life. It said to me that we accept as reality the kind of world we live in and seldom contemplate the possibility that things might be totally different. This is certainly true of our existence in the everyday world we now call "reality." But suppose there are other realities all around us — even an infinite number of realities — that we don't accept as reality because we aren't accustomed to them and perhaps don't even see them at all. Maybe heaven and the life of the Resurrection are a reality present to us even now, though we are too obtuse and buried in everyday reality to see them.

But my conservative and fundamentalist friends won't accept this. They are too literal in their approach to everything. They insist that everything in the Bible is just what it appears to be — that an ax head really did float and the sun really did stand still — and that heaven will be just the way it is described in the Book of Revelation, with walls of jasper, pearly gates, and streets of gold (Revelation 21:15–21). As I said before, they strain at a gnat and swallow a lot of camel dung. They're too busy defending facticity to understand mystery.

Ninth Wrong Teaching

When Bad Things Happen to Good People, There Is Always a Reason

A few years ago Rabbi Harold Kushner wrote an immensely popular book called *When Bad Things Happen to Good People.* The Kushners' son had progeria, a rare disease that causes children to age pathetically while they are still young and to die at an early age. Kushner and his wife had to work through the problem of why God would permit this personal tragedy to occur in their lives. They had both been good people. They were loving parents, and they had been eager for their son's birth. The question of theodicy, or justifying the ways of God, was a natural one for them to raise. Kushner's eventual answer to the dilemma was simple: God doesn't ever send affliction on people. Our suffering is merely part of the price we pay for living in an unfinished world. It is actually an opportunity for us to grow in our understanding of faith.

The church I grew up in did not teach this view of personal tragedy. Instead, it attributed everything to God — even disease, heartbreak, and death. Anything less would have seemed to my conservative and fundamentalist forebears a diminution of the power and sovereignty of the deity.

"God has taken her to be with him," the minister said at the funeral for my nine-year-old sister. I am sure it was comforting to my parents, who were still in shock at her sudden death, and I doubt if they ever reflected on the theology of the remark. It was merely assumed, in the conservative community where we lived, that God ordered the affairs of everybody. "The Lord giveth and the Lord taketh away."

We had a neighbor, a quiet, well-mannered bricklayer all week, but a demon to his wife on Saturday evenings when he got drunk. One night when he was too inebriated to know better, he went to sleep outside in a cold rain, got pneumonia, and died. Everybody said God had done it because of his sins. Some even suggested that he was now going to roast in hell for eternity.

The prevalence of this kind of thinking forced a careful examination of every unfortunate or tragic occurrence in our community for reasons why God was taking action against the victims. When a tornado swept the roof off a huge tobacco warehouse that was only a few months old, people supposed there was some secret in the life of the owner that accounted for what had happened. When a respected citizen was stricken by a muscular disease that left him twisted and wracked by pain the rest of his life, everybody said he must have harbored some dark secret that provoked the Lord against him. When the rakehell son of a popular minister crashed his private airplane into the side of a mountain on a rainy night, it was suggested that God was punishing him for being a thorn in his godly father's side.

Nothing happened by accident. God was always involved in it.

Sometimes people said those who suffered in this life were lucky compared to those who died and went to hell. Hell was very vivid to us in the fundamentalist churches of those days. Every evangelist preached on it, usually on the last night of the revival meeting. The more imaginative preachers tried to improve on Jonathan Edwards, whose famous sermon, "Sinners in the Hands of an Angry God," was filled with frightening descriptions of what would happen to those who didn't grovel before God for salvation. Their stories and imagery were guaranteed to terrify the more sensitive children in the crowd, leaving some with nightmares for weeks to come.

I had twin brothers-in-law who spent three years living in trenches and foxholes in the Philippines during World War II. They returned stateside in 1945 and attended a tent revival meeting in their hometown. The preacher spoke for an hour and a half one night on the terrors of hell. Afterward, one twin began reading his Bible fervently. He carried it around all the time, citing verses about punishment and retribution. Within weeks, he had a nervous breakdown, and his twin followed suit.

If my wife really wants to embarrass me, she recalls the title of a sermon I preached in a youth revival, as it was called, in Monticello, Kentucky. She didn't hear the sermon, I am thankful to say, but she saw the title in a newspaper advertisement. It was "Turn or Burn." I was eighteen years old and was trying to preach on the subjects I felt compelled to address because all the evangelists did it. I am sure it was a terrible sermon, and I am glad I remember nothing of it today.

Today my idea of hell is simply that it is the absence of God, either in this life or in whatever life we experience beyond this one. When Jesus spoke, as he sometimes did, of "fire" and "hellfire" for those who were living morally or spiritually unacceptable lives, I am convinced that his apocalyptic imagination was merely borrowing a convenient image from the rabbinical talk of the time, which often identified the burning of trash with divine retribution for sin. It seems never to have been a very central doctrine for him and certainly doesn't square very well with his prayer from the cross for forgiveness for his enemies or his assurance to the thief who died beside him, "Today you will be with me in paradise."

But in those days I was exposed to a much more strin-

gent opinion. The more vengeful adults in my church loved
consigning people to the fires of hell. The Nazis and Japs
(I seldom heard the more respectful term "Japanese" employed) in World War II were all said to be destined for
hell. So were bootleggers, prostitutes, and bookmakers.
There weren't any "circles" of hell, as Dante had envisioned
them in the *Divine Comedy*, with some people assigned to
more inventively unbearable sections than others, but it
was a serious curse if someone said, "May you burn in the
deepest hell!"

Our pastor as much as suggested that anyone who wasn't a
Baptist was in danger of hellfire — especially Roman Catholics and Campbellites, or members of the Disciples church.
Once, when he made the statement in a sermon that Jews
who had not been converted to Christ would burn in hell,
my wife, then a girl of fourteen, went to him to protest. "My
friend Cookie is a Jew," she said, "and she is a good girl. I
do not believe God would send her to hell." The pastor insisted on the truth of his doctrine and warned my wife that
she must witness to the girl if she wished her to be saved.
We are sure, on reflection, that that encounter marked a
turning point in our pastor's regard for my wife, for a few
years later, when he heard that she and I were engaged, he
drew me aside to suggest that she would not make a good
minister's wife.

UNTIL MODERN TIMES, when human knowledge became
vastly multiplied, we lived in what the sociologists call "an
enchanted world." That is, nothing happened in the world
that was not ordered by some supernatural force, say, a
god or a demon. When a plague broke out, whole cities
turned to prayer and supplication. If a crop was poor, the
farmer doubled his prayers for a good crop the next year.
When tribal hunting was successful, the entire tribe offered
sacrifices of thanksgiving. If a woman was barren, she was

considered sinful and unworthy and being punished by God. Cotton Mather, the prominent New England divine, once wrote in his diary that he had a toothache and must examine his conscience to see what he had done to offend the Almighty.

As modern science began to explain phenomena more satisfactorily, the world ceased to be so enchanted. God became, as philosopher Michael Polanyi once put it, a "God of the gaps," dragged in to explain the events and occurrences for which there was still no rational explanation. The frontiers of sacred power have shrunk steadily over the last few centuries. First we understood why lightning strikes the earth and why there are floods and famine. Then we learned about bacteria and disease. Now we know about DNA and brain disorders and other subtle aspects of human chemistry. And with this loss of enchantment has come a corresponding growth in secularism and agnosticism.

What *is* God's role in a world where cause and effect are so much more visible than they once were and extend to such microscopic dimensions? Deism was the first answer to this. Following on the heels of Newtonian physics, deists responded by positing a universe set in motion like a clock, with rules of causality so finely fixed in its nature that the immediate attendance of the deity was no longer required to make it operate. But deism provided a lonely universe where people were hungry for a more intimate relationship to God, and evangelical Christianity exerted a greater appeal than the cold logicality of a more rational religion.

Now the heirs of evangelical Christianity — the conservatives and fundamentalists — have become more or less dominant in American religion, and they still insist that God is vitally interested in everything we do at the personal level: in the books we read, the way we talk to our children, the money we have in the bank, the kind of new car we buy, the place where we go to spend our vacation. "Pray about everything," say the preachers of this high-intimacy faith. "Don't undertake anything without first checking with God."

They are not alone in this, of course. The sense that God is all-invasive, that nothing we do escapes divine notice, has never really left us. When President Wilson's wife died in 1914, he said, "God has stricken me almost beyond the point which I can bear." Wilson was a university professor and president, a sophisticated citizen of the world. Yet he reflected in his personal thinking the residuum of Calvinistic theology that has never fully faded from the American mind.

Dr. Jimmy Allen, the minister I mentioned in chapter six, whose daughter-in-law and grandchildren had AIDS, wrote of the older grandchild in 1995, "In my weakest moments, I wondered why God would allow such a great kid as Matt to be born, only to take him away from us." He said he was helped by an article written by Michael Gartner in his *USA Today* column about the sudden death of his seventeen-year-old son. Gartner cited a conversation with a friend who helped him deal with the brevity of his son's life. The friend said, "If God had come to you seventeen years ago and said, 'I'll make you a bargain. I'll give you a beautiful, wonderful, happy kid for seventeen years and then I'll take him away,' you would have made that deal in a second."[29]

I confess that I myself am not free of such thinking. When each of our sons went through a painful divorce, I often awoke in the night wondering, "Why, God?" My wife is a wonderful pianist and organist and loves to practice by the hour. Now that she is in her midsixties, her knuckles are becoming swollen and deformed by arthritis. Wincing at the sight of her hands and the thought of her pain, I say, "Oh God, why?" And sometimes in the night, when I myself am experiencing a toothache or an impacted sinus cavity, I will promise God to praise him if he will only take away the excruciating pain.

It is all very confusing. I know with my head that God

has nothing to do with the pains and tragedies we suffer in human existence. He certainly does not cause them. He is not like Cetebos, in Robert Browning's poem, "Caliban upon Cetebos," a primitive deity that Caliban imagines to be as capricious as himself, watching twenty crabs crawling by and stoning the twenty-first. He doesn't have a barrel of measles and a barrel of whooping-cough by his throne from which he dispenses punishments on children who have been unkind to their pets or spoken contentiously to their parents. We live in a world of natural causality and random disaster, and the God of Jesus is not to be blamed for the "slings and arrows of outrageous fortune" we suffer. I know that. The world is no longer enchanted. Things simply happen. The good can experience pain and rejection as easily as the bad can enjoy comfort and reward.

Yet I was formed from childhood to "take it to the Lord in prayer," and to believe that not a sparrow falls without his noticing and caring. It is hard not to think in terms of reward and retribution. The very universe itself is supposed to be moral, punishing the guilty and elevating the just. "Truth crushed to earth," and all of that. How shall I resolve the dilemma? I wish the church of my childhood had had a maturer approach to the limitations of our humanity and had equipped me with a different set of responses when I encounter suffering. If only it had cared less about the glory and sovereignty of God and more about the love of God, I think I would not now live with such ambivalence.

As I MENTIONED in chapter two, my wife and I recently visited the Holocaust Memorial in Washington, D.C. It was a difficult experience. In room after room, we saw the photographs of Jewish people — not merely in masses, but individuals — who had been sent to Hitler's work camps or to chemical ovens where they died as thick as sardines in a can because it would have been a waste of gas not to crowd them in as closely as possible. There were pictures of Jews being subjected to the most horrible medical experiments — including women with hooks in their breasts — by doctors who were as cruel as their masters in the Third Reich. Little children stared at the camera with dark, unblinking eyes, wondering what would happen next in the nightmare they were living.

Two experiences in the memorial haunt our memories. One is the railroad boxcar through which we passed. It was smaller than I imagined the boxcars would have been. Standing inside it, I thought of the poor, frightened, disoriented Jews forced into such claustrophobic quarters for the long, slow rides to the camps. There were no sanitary provisions. People simply urinated and defecated in their clothing. There was no room for personal belongings. Those were men, women, and children suddenly deprived of everything, even their dignity, and shuttled off to the most horrible experiences that could befall human beings. There was no one else in the boxcar when we walked through it, yet I felt myself suffocating, needing to get out where the air was cleaner and more refreshing.

The other experience was in the hall of shoes. The passageway proceeds between two areas filled with discarded shoes of Jewish victims. Most are grayish in appearance. The laces are all gone. The Nazis probably had some use for them, perhaps in the shoes of the soldiers who fought on the front lines of the war. There are all kinds of shoes — men's, women's, children's — in many sizes, though on average they are smaller than shoes today. The pairs were long ago separated. Now they lie there, inert and ownerless, wingtips, working shoes, and walking shoes all churned together. On one side of the passageway I saw a red pump. The heel was not very high — perhaps two inches — but it was clearly a dress shoe.

I thought of the woman who had worn it and wondered

if she had been to a party where there was joy and laughter, where friends' voices floated in the air and there was a spirit of warmth and compassion. Was she excited when she bought the shoes? Did she carry them home and show them proudly to her husband, saying she would wear them to such-and-such affair?

There was no laughter in the hall of shoes. There were only echoes of the voices of those poor people rounded up in the night and herded off to the camps. I wondered if the woman with the red pumps was taken from the party, for wouldn't she have worn something more sensible if she had had any idea where she was going? The people were lucky who were in their work shoes or walking shoes, for those would be much more serviceable in forced marches or while standing long hours every day at factory workbenches.

It was all so heart-wrenchingly sad, so terribly pathetic. I felt, as I left the museum, the way I'm sure many Jews felt leaving it, and many others have felt, even back in the war years themselves: Where was God in all of this? Was this a punishment on the Jewish people for not recognizing the Messiah when he came almost two thousand years ago? Rubbish! I cannot believe that, even for a minute. I cannot accept that even a conservative or fundamentalist could believe such a thing of God.

Years ago I met Professor Richard Rubenstein at a university colloquium where we were both speaking. At the time, he was teaching at Florida State University in Tallahassee and working on a book about the Jewish experience. We had several conversations. He had become an atheist, he said, because of what his people had suffered at Auschwitz and Buchenwald and all the other camps. At the time, I was disappointed, even appalled, to hear him say this. Surely faith is supposed to rally above all life's misfortunes. But now I understand. Six million people is a lot of punishment. Especially the little children. I am like Ivan Karamazov, in

Dostoevsky's novel, and Albert Camus, the French writer —
it is the torture and death of innocent children I would lay
at God's doorstep with the note, "What do you have to say
about this?"

More than I have recognized, the Holocaust convinced
me that God is not personally involved in people's suffering — at least not in any way we have imagined him to be.
There is a line in Archibald MacLeish's *J.B.,* the verse play
about the biblical character Job, that contains great wisdom.
J.B. is speaking to his wife, Sarah, trying to get her to be less
hard on the deity:

> God is there too, in the desperation.
> I do not know why God should strike
> But God is what is stricken also.[30]

God doesn't inflict punishment on human beings. It
merely happens. Sometimes it is the result of collective
cruelty and insanity, as in the case of the Jews in the Holocaust. But God isn't to blame. And neither must God be
expected to rescue us from such situations. God is not an
omnipotent figure capable of ordering either punishment
or rescue. God suffers with the creation, the way a father suffers with his AIDS-stricken children or grandchildren. There
may be comfort in that. But God does not visit with affliction
or rescue from it.

Rabbi Kushner says in *When Bad Things Happen to Good
People* that Christianity introduced the idea of a God who
suffers along with his children and that postbiblical Judaism
took up the notion of a God who went into exile with his
people and wept with them there.

> I don't know what it means for God to suffer. I don't
> believe that God is a person like me, with real eyes and
> real tear ducts to cry, and real nerve endings to feel
> pain. But I would like to think that the anguish I feel

when I read of the sufferings of innocent people reflects God's anguish and God's compassion, even if His way of feeling pain is different from ours. I would like to think that He is the source of my being able to feel sympathy and outrage, and that He and I are on the same side when we stand with the victim against those who would hurt him.[31]

In the end, our Buddhist and Hindu friends may be right, that human suffering is not as important as we sometimes make it out to be, and that we must simply learn to endure it, to ignore and rise above it whenever possible, but when we cannot, merely endure it. It is true, in some cases at least, that suffering is ennobling, that it purifies the soul and prepares us for chaster thoughts and conceptions of living. Long, grueling pain or discomfort is probably demeaning as well as debilitating, but even that, as some have managed to demonstrate, can be borne with grace and dignity.

I do not mean to sound callous. But I often fear there is a kind of self-centered "whinyness" besetting many people today, including Christians. Life has been soft for many of us, and we forget the hardships our ancestors regularly endured. Perhaps we need to abstract ourselves from our situations enough to gain a nobler perspective. Christians in particular should be able to respond to life with more toughness and resiliency, for presumably we still believe in a life to come that transcends pain and suffering. What did St. Paul say? "I consider that the sufferings of this present time are not worth comparing with the glory about to be revealed to us" (Romans 8:18).

If we were more concerned about the welfare of others and the preservation of our planet and the simple companionship of God, we would not worry as much as we presently do about our health, our comfort, and our prosperity. We would adopt a more sacrificial attitude, asking, when pain or difficulty comes, not "Why me?" but "Why not me?"

In the video narration at the end of the pilgrimage through the Holocaust Memorial, a survivor recalls talking with a friend of his who was about to go to his prayers and give thanks to God. "Why would you do that?" he asked his friend. "Look at the mess we are in. How can you thank God at a time like this?" The friend reminded him of what their persecutors were like. Between them and us, he said, I would rather be us. "I will thank God that we are not like them," he said.

ONE OF THE PROBLEMS with rejecting the idea that God intervenes personally in our lives, ordering rewards and punishments and even death, is that it calls into question the validity of intercessory prayer. A God who isn't intimately involved in our existence wouldn't be much help when called upon.

If conservatives believe anything, they believe that God hears and answers their prayers. How many times in my youth did I hear sermons on "Ask, and ye shall receive" (Matthew 7:7 KJV) and "If ye have faith as a grain of mustard seed, ye shall say unto this mountain, Remove hence to yonder place, and it shall remove; and nothing shall be impossible unto you" (Matthew 17:20 KJV). If we prayed and didn't see results, there was never any question about whether God heard the prayer or had the power to grant our petitions. The failure was always in us. We didn't have enough faith, or we didn't ask what it was in God's will to grant.

I prayed very fervently in those years. I asked God to make my father a Christian and to give my mother the happiness I thought she deserved. I prayed that I would find God's will and have the strength to follow it. I asked for a loving companion for my life. I think I was about as unwavering in my faith as it was possible to be. I used to sing the little chorus "Got Any Rivers":

Got any rivers you think are uncrossable?
Got any mountains you cannot tunnel through?
God specializes in things that seem impossible;
He knows a thousand ways to make a way for you.

Eventually, I believe all those prayers were answered, especially the one for companionship. I could not have dreamed of having a finer, more loving wife than the woman I married; I continue each day to marvel at her grace and attractiveness, and to give thanks for the way our lives have become happily intertwined across the years. I believe my mother was a happy woman in her latter decades. My father had not become a Christian and continued to be as self-centered and dominant as ever. But she was so accommodating that they managed to achieve a workable peace in their marriage and in their last few years did almost everything together.

Perhaps the greatest miracle of all was my father's reported conversion in his final months of life. He had been reduced in circumstances, his failing health having restricted him to a nursing home and necessitated frequent trips to the hospital. A neighbor proved a faithful friend during those months, visiting him in the nursing home and running little errands for him. The neighbor was a deacon in my home church and always reported to me anything he thought I might want to know. One time, he said, he had stood at the door of my father's room at the nursing home and heard him moaning and praying for forgiveness. Another time, he said my father had confessed to him what a selfish man he had always been, but that God had saved him.

Something very strange occurred as we were burying my father. He had not been a member of the church, so we had only a graveside service, which I myself conducted. It was a warm, beautiful day in April. The sky was vividly blue. Not a leaf was stirring on the trees. But as I began to pray a final prayer over my father's coffin, an icy wind began to blow, toppling several vases of flowers and whipping the flaps of the funeral tent. Two or three men held to the tent poles to avoid being blown over, and their coats were standing out at right angles. Hail pelted the tent and the ground around us. I had to raise my voice to be heard above the din. I felt strangely as if the devil were battling for my father's soul and that I had to resist with all my might. Then, as suddenly as the tempest had begun, it abated. The skies cleared and everything seemed normal again.

Afterward, several friends and relatives spoke of the remarkable thing that had happened. They had all felt very tense, they said, for the occurrence seemed to them little short of supernatural. Even some people who are not very religious by nature admitted that they thought we were engaged in some kind of contest over my father's eternal destination, and that in the end he had been permitted to enter heaven by the skin of his teeth.

I also believe, over the years, that I have found God's will for my life and continued to follow it. I recognize its authenticity by the very difficulties paving the road. Several times, following God's will has meant uprooting from a place where my family and I were quite comfortable, to undertake something new or different that would prove challenging and unpleasant. Of six major changes in position I accepted across my life as a minister and teacher, in three I took a reduction in pay. Now, in semiretirement, I look back over the way I have come and embrace it all, even the move to Samford University that proved so disappointing.

So in a way I have to say that my prayers from those early years were all answered, and I am deeply humbled by that realization. And there have been significant times in my life since then when I believe I have seen answers to prayers for my family and for people in my congregations. But there have also been many prayers not answered, especially for the health and well-being of some people very dear to me.

I think of my friend Jack Cosby, the dear man responsible for my coming to Lynchburg's First Presbyterian Church. Jack's brother, Gordon, founded the Church of the Savior in Washington, D.C. It was Gordon's wife, Mary, who telephoned Jack after she and I had appeared on a program at a United Methodist pastors' conference in Macon, Georgia, and suggested me as a candidate for his church's ministry. He was chairman of the search committee, and one of the sincerest, most unaffected people I ever met. I tried to say no before I had even prayed about going to Lynchburg, but I couldn't do it because Jack was so irresistible.

While we were in Lynchburg, Jack suffered a terrible blow. He had been president of a savings and loan institution started by his father. It was during the volatile days of the 1980s, when interest rates were at 16 percent and banks were making a lot of unsecured loans. Jack committed to a big loan in Texas that eventually failed and cost the company a lot of money. Some board members Jack had appointed and whom he trusted as good friends betrayed him and made him the scapegoat for the institution's entire spate of difficulties, which ran far beyond the Texas loan. They confronted him without warning at a board meeting and demanded that he resign and clean out his desk immediately.

Brokenhearted at the betrayal and subsequent disgrace in the community, Jack courageously soldiered on, becoming a traveling representative for some novelty companies selling products to gift stores. His wife, extremely hurt by what had happened, wanted to move to their lake home and sell their town property, which was adjacent to Jack's parents' old home. Jack couldn't part with the property, but they did sell a lot of antiques to meet financial obligations. Their two sons married. One failed in business and the other had a child born nearly blind. The latter also had testicular cancer and underwent an operation. His wife asked for a divorce. Then Jack himself had cancer and underwent surgery and extensive chemotherapy. Through it all, Job-like, he kept his faith in God and attempted to live as faithfully and cheerfully as possible.

I was deeply distressed by Jack's suffering. He was one of the finest men I had ever known. He certainly did not deserve the catalog of woes that befell him. I prayed every day for his well-being, first as he dealt with his release from the loan company, then as he worked as a salesman and faced his children's problems, and finally as he went in and out of hospital with the cancer that took his life. At no point in the process did I feel that my prayers availed anything. I do not believe they were even responsible for Jack's keeping his faith in God, for that was innate in the man. His wonderful mother had instilled unconquerable faith and love in all her children, and it was this that sustained him during his horrible ordeal. I drew a complete zero on my efforts to turn things around for Jack through prayer. So did many others. Either God didn't choose to intervene or he couldn't.

Many other times in my life I have prayed fervently for things that weren't given. I used to pray daily for all the homeless people who lived around our church in Los Angeles. There were often sixty or seventy of them lined up for help by the time I got to the church in the morning. But I couldn't even persuade the board of trustees at the church to set up a series of portable toilets for them in our parking lots. "Too dangerous," they said. "Lawsuits, and all that."

I prayed for our dear friend, Chuck Jones, to be relieved of his painful colon cancer and restored to health. Chuck was a lovely gay man, a talented musician and decorator, and when we moved to Birmingham he flew there to help us decorate our new home. He was as sweet and sensitive as anybody I have ever known. But Chuck died a slow and horrible death, and my prayers for him were of no avail.

I prayed for our sons and their wives when they were going through their divorces, that somehow they could all be happy and have the kind of wonderful, supportive relationship my wife and I have enjoyed all these years, but it didn't happen. They still divorced, and there were hard feelings, and it has taken a long time for the wounds to heal.

I don't blame the conservative church I came out of for not having sorted these things out and handed me some easier answers. There may not be any answers — at least none we can understand in this life. But I do think part of the responsibility for the confusion I have to live with may be laid at the door of the church's stubborn adherence to the omnipotence of God and the idea that God controls everything about our lives, from the acne we get as teenagers to the time and manner in which we die.

Rabbi Kushner offers some important insights in a chapter called "God Can't Do Everything, but He Can Do Some Important Things." Praying for people's health or the outcome of an operation, he says, has "implications that ought to disturb a thoughtful person. If prayer worked the way many people think it does, no one would ever die, because no prayer is ever offered more sincerely than the prayer for life, for health and recovery from illness, for ourselves and for those we love."[32] When we pray earnestly for worthwhile results but see none, we are moved to ask why our prayers were not answered. This may well lead to feelings of guilt or anger or even hopelessness.

If we acknowledge that God doesn't always answer the prayers of good people with the finest motivations, says Kushner, there is one alternative to giving up on prayer: "We can change our understanding of what it means to pray, and what it means for our prayers to be answered."[33]

I will always pray about the things that mean most to me —
friends, loved ones, values, organizations, personal desires.
I can't help it. After all these years it is simply inbred in
me. But I can refuse to ask for a parking space, which some
conservative preachers claim solves the parking problem for
anyone who will do it, and to believe that God exercises
fastidious control over the events surrounding our passage
from this life. Instead, I shall aim at a kind of selfless spirituality in which I try to accept as gallantly as possible whatever
happens to me and others, and to praise God, like the poor
man in the Holocaust, that life is as well arranged as it is.

In the end, the most intelligent prayer a Christian can
make may well be the one our Lord offered in the garden of
Gethsemane, "not my will, but thine be done." This avoids all
the small commitments in favor of one huge one, and it describes a genuinely humble stance. It leaves God's manner of
working in the realms of mystery, which is appropriate, and
implies a fierce submission on our part to whatever power
God may have and however God may choose to use it.

I AM MUCH INDEBTED to Brother David Steindl-Rast, a member of a Benedictine monastery in Elmira, New York, for
his book *Gratefulness, the Heart of Prayer.* The spiritual life,
Steindl-Rast suggests, is really about the ability of our souls
to be surprised, to see the wonder in things. Sluggish, we
often fail to see or be surprised. We take everything for
granted. But when our spirits are properly aroused, we begin
to marvel at things. Sunsets, dandelions, the songs of birds,
the texture of skin, children playing in a neighboring yard,
the voices of people speaking in a language they mutually
understand. Everything becomes a catalyst, an opening to
the sense of worship.

Steindl-Rast describes one of his personal catalysts, a beautiful cardinal that returns almost daily to the food he spreads
for it:

No matter how often that cardinal comes for the cracked corn scattered on a rock for the birds in winter, it is a flash of surprise. I expect him. I've come to even know his favorite feeding times. I can hear him chirping long before he comes in sight. But when that red streak shoots down on the rock like lightning on Elijah's altar, I know what e.e. cummings means: "The eyes of my eyes are opened."[34]

When we reach this stage of amazement, we cease to desire things for ourselves. The world is already more than we can take in. It is abundant with miracles and infinitely capable of sustaining our joy. Instead of asking God for this or that — all the things we wished before we acquired the sense of wonder — we want to praise him for the wealth that surrounds us. Thanksgiving becomes the heart and soul of devotion. Death, says Steindl-Rast, actually lies behind us, not before us. Now we are open to life, whatever happens.

For me, there is enormous truth in this. It speaks to my conundrum about how to pray when I no longer believe God visits us with rewards and punishments or calls us home when the time has come. There is a stage of faith beyond that of seeing God's hand in people's misfortunes and deaths. It is the stage where we see and feel the holy presence everywhere, as much in the dew on the summer grass as in the illness suffered by our bodies. When we reach the place where we simply marvel at everything and live attentive to the constant displays of divine creativity around us, we worship continually, even in the face of disaster.

In his deeply moving book *Man's Search for Meaning,* Viktor Frankl described how even the Jews incarcerated and abused by the Nazis managed at times to see the wonder of God's universe. Once, at the end of a hard day of labor when the men were lying exhausted on their bunks, someone came running inside and urged them all to come out quickly into the courtyard. When they stood outside, they could see the sun shining red and purple in a large puddle of water standing in the center of the yard. They all stood reverently before it, beholding a miracle in the midst of their enormous suffering.

This is for me a much more meaningful stance toward the deity than the one I learned from my conservative church. What God does and how he does it is still a profound mystery to me. I am such a dullard, such an imbecile about things. But I can tell that he made the world and is still working on it, that his presence in it is the most amazing thing my tiny human mind can ever perceive. I will continue to offer prayers for my brothers and sisters, and when I am weak and cannot help it, even for myself. But whether they are answered or not does not matter, for the world is still so beautiful that I shall stand in awe of him forever.

Tenth Wrong Teaching

Conservatives Want Everybody to Be Free

Freedom is one of the big myths among conservatives and fundamentalists. Pastors brag about the freedom of the pulpit. They talk a lot about "soul freedom" and "freedom of conscience," implying that these items are practically guaranteed among their churches but are in dangerously short supply among moderates and liberals. The so-called "liberal establishment" that they are always decrying supposedly brainwashes its members and robs them of their individuality before God. God has given us freedom of choice, they are always insisting, and we must be careful to use it.

I was gullible and believed all this, until the Missions Conference at Golden Gate Theological Seminary I mentioned in the introduction to this book. The seminary hosts such a conference every year — or did at the time of my visit — as a means of bringing hundreds of potential students to its campus. There were eight hundred that year, and the seminary, which sits on prime real estate overlooking the Bay north of San Francisco, regarded the conference as one of the year's most important meetings. I was considered a "hot" young preacher Southern Baptists were proud to have on the faculty at Vanderbilt Divinity School. I had spoken the year before at Ridgecrest Baptist Assembly, the denomination's enormous "camp" in the mountains of North Carolina, and was considered a hit. When I flew to San Francisco, I had already been engaged to preach the next summer at Ridgecrest and also at Glorieta, the denomination's other big camp in New Mexico.

The program was carefully planned. I was even assigned topics on which to speak: "Christ in a World in Revolution" and "Christ *Is* a Revolution." I could handle that. It was the midsixties, and revolution was in the air. The themes excited me. As requested, I wrote the addresses and submitted them to the seminary's administration well in advance, ostensibly for reprinting and for providing juicy quotes to various newspapers and journals.

It was my first visit to California, and I was duly impressed. I stayed in the home of a faculty member from Kentucky who had known my mother when they were young. I was wined and dined by the preaching professor, a former North Carolina minister named Winston Pearce. "Wined and dined" must be understood as a figure of speech — Baptists in official positions never drink wine in public. We visited bayside restaurants in Sausalito and had delightful chats about life and preaching as we watched sailboats gliding romantically by the docks where we dined.

My first address to the enthusiastic crowd of college students went exceptionally well. That was on Saturday evening. On Sunday morning I gave the second address. I talked about Christ as a free man and how contagious real freedom is. In the course of the address I made forty-five seconds worth of parenthetic remarks about something I had discerned since moving to Nashville, where the Baptist Sunday School Board is located. I had many friends at the board, I said, and they all had distinctive personalities. Yet everything they wrote for denominational publications sounded alike. Either they were not free to say what they really thought, or what they said had been edited to eliminate any differences of opinion. Many of the young people before me, I knew, would end up being pastors, missionaries, and denominational officials. I wanted them to be aware of this bowdlerizing tendency at the board so they could combat it and keep the denomination free.

I noticed Professor Pearce moving over behind the president of the seminary, Harold Graves, and speaking to him. Later I learned that he was saying, "Will you get up and refute him or must I?" I did not know what a firestorm of controversy I had ignited. The seminary was coming up for its annual allocation from the Baptist Sunday School Board — a thousand dollars for every student it enrolled — and a representative of the board was present. The president was under fire from fundamentalists on the West Coast for not being hard-line enough with his faculty. He had also been caught recently trying to manipulate the hiring of a favorite candidate for the pastorate of the large Baptist church nearest the seminary.

When I sat down to the applause of the students, President Graves followed me to the pulpit. During seven or eight minutes of inarticulate fumbling, he tried to dissociate the seminary from my remarks. Several times he repeated the phrase, "we *are* free, we *are* free." While he was attempting to sanitize the seminary in the eyes of the board representative who was there, he had some associates in the reception hall below the chapel confiscating the eight hundred copies of my address the seminary had duplicated to hand out to the attendees, and also the copies of the audiotapes some student engineers had been making. I have always been amused by the irony of the combination — his insistence on total freedom and the totalitarian tactics regarding the tapes and addresses.

I was shaken by this act of refutation. I had never experienced such a reaction to my speaking and never would again. I felt especially embarrassed before my hosts for the visit — my mother's old friends — for I sensed I had brought opprobrium upon their house. They said very little about what had happened, as if it were too painful to talk about, and there was a kind of shadow over our relationship. My wife said I came home pale and upset.

But that was not the end of the matter. President Graves was coming to Nashville the following week for a meeting of the Executive Board of the denomination. He brought along one of the confiscated tapes and played it for the board. I was not aware of this at the time, of course, or of Dr. James Sullivan's call — he was executive secretary of the Southern Baptist Convention — to the vice-chancellor of Vanderbilt University asking that I be dismissed from my job.

The next thing I was aware of was a telephone call from Dr. Sullivan asking if I could come down to the board building to meet with him. I said I would be happy to do that and asked when. He said it needed to be right then, late on Friday afternoon, as he was leaving the next day for the Philippines and would not return for two or three weeks. I said I was sorry, but my wife was out shopping, I was alone caring for our youngest child, and we had only the car my wife was using. Frustrated, he asked if he could come to see me at home. I agreed. I should have known, considering how busy he was and that he was willing to make a house call, what an important confrontation was about to take place.

For thirty minutes, Dr. Sullivan sat in our den and insisted that I retract the remarks I had made about the lack of freedom at the Sunday School Board. Perhaps I was more stubborn than I should have been, but I failed to see a good reason for doing what he asked. I was convinced of the truth of the remarks and had been raised to believe that Baptists were a free people who could call things exactly as they saw them. Dr. Sullivan's voice grew more and more shrill, and once or twice he shocked me by interjecting the word "damn" in the conversation. Finally he said I should at least agree to come to the board for one of its meetings and observe the board in action, when I would see that I was wrong and it was indeed free in its manner of acting. I said I would be glad to do this, with one provision: that I could bring with me a couple of former board workers I knew who could substantiate whether what I was seeing was a normal meeting or one modified for my inspection. This made him very angry, and he left the house in what I could only characterize as an unfriendly spirit.

I thought this would be the last of an unpleasant matter. At least I did not intend to pursue it further. Then I saw a schedule in a denominational magazine of the weeks at Ridgecrest and Glorieta when I was supposed to be there, and my name wasn't on the program. I went to the person at the Sunday School Board in charge of the schedule. He admitted that I had been cancelled from the programs. I asked for a letter officially telling me that I was not welcome. He said he could not give me one. I had simply been "evaporated."

I learned also of an energetic campaign President Graves had waged against me in California. At a faculty meeting he called on Monday morning, Graves attempted to get the entire faculty to sign a statement denouncing me as a troublemaker. Almost all the faculty members had missed the presentation on Sunday morning, as they were out preaching in various churches, and they counseled against enlarging the matter by calling further attention to it.

Angry with the faculty, Graves drove to Sacramento to meet with Dr. Terry Young, editor of the California Baptist newspaper. The next week there was a large front-page article in that paper about my careless remarks at the conference and a long editorial by Young accusing me of being immoral and untrustworthy. The charge of immorality stemmed from my having used an illustration from James Baldwin's novel *Giovanni's Room*. Baldwin, as everybody knew — or would know after the publication of the editorial — was a black homosexual writer from New York.

One irate faculty member from the seminary, Dr. James

McClendon, telephoned when the paper appeared and urged me to bring a lawsuit against Graves, Young, and the California Baptist paper. In retrospect, I think I should have followed his advice. At the time, I was still reeling from the experience of denominational rejection and shrank from taking fellow Christians to court.

Soon my wife and I began to notice that our friends who worked at the board were not speaking to us. Even in the church we attended, they pretended not to see us when we passed. We tried phoning some of our closest friends at the board and inviting them to dinner. We knew they would come for dinner, for my wife is a wonderful cook and they always enjoyed coming. But now they were all busy. The ostracism continued for two years. Eventually a friend confided that they all understood they would be fired if seen with us.

While all of this grieved us at the time, we look back now and are grateful for the gift these former friends bestowed on us. They gave us a wonderful excuse to leave the Baptist church. We went on a sabbatical leave to Europe. When we returned, we joined Vine Street Christian Church, Disciples of Christ, where my wife became the junior choir director.

A year or two later, a Baptist Student Union director from Berea College in Kentucky was on the Vanderbilt campus. "I heard you patched it up with Dr. Sullivan and the board," he said. I raised an eyebrow. "You didn't?" he asked. He told me this story: a vice-president from Golden Gate Baptist Theological Seminary had been on the Berea campus recently to recruit students. At a meeting, one of the students asked, "What about the Killinger affair?" "Oh, Dr. Killinger and Dr. Sullivan have ironed all that out," the vice-president responded with alacrity. "Dr. Sullivan gave a dinner at the board, at which Dr. Killinger apologized and withdrew his comments. He wept openly before the crowd, and then he and Dr. Sullivan embraced."

I couldn't believe it! What kind of people was I dealing with?

I began to be very cautious around conservatives and fundamentalists who talk about freedom, and to wonder exactly what they mean by it.

PERHAPS I WOULD NOT HAVE BEEN so upset by all this if I had remembered my friend Ted Clark — Dr. Theodore Clark, a professor of theology at New Orleans Baptist Theological Seminary. I met Ted at Harvard when I was working on my basic theological degree and he was spending a year's sabbatical there to study under the great Paul Tillich. Ted's wife, Lois, was a schoolteacher, so had not been able to accompany him on the sabbatical. When I learned this, I invited Ted to have Thanksgiving with us.

My wife and I both loved Ted. He was a tall, gentle man with a kind and thoughtful demeanor. I'll never forget that Thanksgiving afternoon. It was a cold, blustery day, and we had a roaring fire in the parsonage living room. After a big dinner about one o'clock, we all retired to the living room and watched the fire as we listened to music on the radio. We talked about life and families, and in the course of the conversation I urged Ted to go into my study and telephone Lois. He came back visibly buoyed by having spoken to her. We watched a ball game on TV for a little while, and then he fell asleep in his chair. The whole weekend was delightful.

A couple of years later, when I was teaching at Georgetown College in Kentucky, we drove down to spend the Easter holiday with Ted and Lois. The odometer on our old Chrysler clicked over a hundred thousand miles on the trip, and I hung a cloth from the radio antenna and took a picture of it that we still have. Ted was visibly upset when we arrived. We thought maybe there had been a death in the family. No, he assured us, it wasn't as bad as that.

But he was going to have to leave us for part of the afternoon. He was being interrogated by the seminary's board of trustees.

Shortly after being at Harvard, Ted had published a book called *Saved by His Life*. It was a book on soteriology, or the theology of salvation. The principal argument of the book was that it is the entire business of the Incarnation that constitutes the basis for our salvation, not merely Christ's death on the cross. The motto of the book was Romans 5:10 — "For if while we were enemies, we were reconciled to God through the death of his Son, much more surely, having been reconciled, will we be saved by his life."

Someone in the seminary — Ted was never sure if it was Dr. Leo Eddleman, the president, or a board member or one of the faculty members — accused Ted of heresy, saying he was slighting the importance of Christ's crucifixion for our sins. He had been summoned to Eddleman's office for a conference. Eddleman pretended to be his friend and assured him the investigation was benign and everything would be okay. Somebody probably suspected him because he had studied under Tillich, whose theology was questionable because he was an existentialist. Ted was a simple man and believed him.

But if Ted had been sober before the meeting, he was shell-shocked afterward. He couldn't talk to us about it when he first came home, but went into the bedroom with Lois. We could hear them whispering, and realized the news must be bad. Ted told us at dinner that night: the trustees had demanded his resignation. He was crestfallen. Later, when he moved from the denial stage to the anger stage, he said he should have worn a copy of his book on a chain around his neck when he entered the board room, like an albatross of bad luck. But that evening he was clearly beaten. How could those men, most of them pastors and educators, have misunderstood so completely? How could they have repaid his fidelity and hard work as a professor with such willful twisting of his intent?

A YEAR AFTER TED WAS FIRED at New Orleans, another Baptist professor became the center of a much bigger controversy. His name was Ralph Elliott, and his trouble also centered on a book. Elliott taught at Midwestern Baptist Theological Seminary in Kansas City. He had been invited by the editors of Broadman Press, the Southern Baptist Convention's official publishing arm, to write a commentary on the Book of Genesis for a new commentary series on the Bible. The editors surely knew that Genesis was a tricky book for a Baptist professor to write about. If the book had any heft at all in scholarly circles, it had to acknowledge the documentary hypothesis endorsed by most Old Testament experts, which contends that Genesis was not written by Moses at all, as tradition had it, but by two or more writers whose works had been conjoined by a third writer or redactor. Elliott didn't make a big to-do about the authorship question, but he did deal with it forthrightly. It wasn't long before the fundamentalists in the denomination were screaming for his head.

The president of Midwestern Seminary, Millard Berquist, was at first supportive of Elliott, as were a number of Elliott's former colleagues at Southern Baptist Theological Seminary in Louisville. But as the controversy worsened, Berquist started distancing himself from Elliott "for the sake of saving the institution."[35] Various colleagues likewise weakened. Even Elliott's mentor and supervisor at Southern Seminary, Professor Clyde T. Francisco, supported him only faintheartedly, and ended by actually "fanning the flames of hostility"[36] against him.

Driven out of the Southern Baptist Convention, Elliott eventually found refuge as pastor of an American Baptist church in New York State. He has since claimed that what he went through with the fundamentalists in the early 1960s was a foretaste of the militant takeover of the SBC in later years, and the if people had stood firmly against the fundamentalists then, the fundamentalists might not control the denomination today.

I'M SURE MY SHOCK at what happened to me after the addresses at Golden Gate Seminary stemmed in part from my upbringing in the Baptist church, where we were constantly assured of the sanctity of individual opinion. Unlike Roman Catholics, who had no choice but to accept the doctrines of their church and pronouncements of their pope, we Baptists were the heirs of a great tradition of dissent, going back to the left wing of the Reformation and the term "Anabaptist," a derisive name given to those who insisted that they be rebaptized as true believers because they could not accept the false baptism of their infancy. Roger Williams, banished from the Massachusetts Bay Colony for opposing religious coercion, founded Providence, Rhode Island, as a haven for nonconformists and was a member of the first Baptist church in America, established in 1639. The Baptist heritage was one of openness, challenge, and individuality, and I took this very seriously.

Too seriously, apparently. I thought, in voicing my opinions in the Golden Gate addresses, that I was upholding a precious tradition. I believed I was contributing to the vitality of that tradition by calling people's attention to places where the tradition was being violated. What I did not realize is that in any church or organization there are always *two* traditions, the mythological tradition, which is rich and noble and gives the organization its pride in itself, and the practical tradition, tacitly agreed upon by the leaders and others in positions of power, which is sometimes treacherous and ignoble, but quite useful to members of the organization who are of a Machiavellian inclination. In upholding the first tradition, I had unwittingly crossed the battlelines of the second and had to be dealt with quickly and severely.

I have since given a lot of thought to the coexistence of these two traditions and feel sad that things have to be this way. It lies at the heart of almost any institution's problems. Take the massive predicament of the Catholic Church over pedophilia, for example, which has erupted so publicly in 2002. Many are astounded at the depth and magnitude of the problem, and some have even wondered if the Catholic Church in America will survive the controversy. What has really been exposed by all the publicity is the double tradition in the church. On one hand, there is the centuries-old authority and dignity of the church of St. Peter, which continues even today to draw many adherents searching for identification with the oldest and most authentic form of Western Christianity. This is the tradition of solemnity and spirituality that boasts all the great figures in Catholic history, such as Benedict, Anselm, Hildegard, Francis of Assisi, Dominic, Catherine of Siena, Julian of Norwich, Ignatius of Loyola, Cardinal Newman, G. K. Chesterton, and Thomas Merton. On the other hand, there is the church's shadow side, the long history of politics and intrigue, by which the Vatican has always maneuvered to control its mighty empire, an empire that has at times rivaled and even enjoyed more power than the world's secular empires. All the cover-ups for the priests who molested children were simply the second tradition's taking over to preserve itself. The cardinals and archbishops who knew about the cover-up, and indeed facilitated it, doubtless rationalized their actions by telling themselves it was for the sake of the first tradition. But it really wasn't. The second tradition almost invariably becomes the operative one in any institution.

The two traditions are constantly at war with one another, even though most people are unaware of their opposition. It is what happened, for example, in the great brouhaha over the multi-denominational Re-Imagining Conference, held in Minneapolis in 1993. An international gathering, sponsored by three separate ecumenical agencies in Minnesota, the conference was devoted to rethinking and redefining traditional faith. Led primarily by women (there was one man on the fifteen-member advisory committee), it sought through imaginative liturgies and presentations to reconceive what Christianity has always been about. Doing this meant that it used a number of new or unfamiliar forms, such as addressing God as the feminine Sophia, or Wisdom personified, as the biblical wisdom literature does.

Response to the conference from traditionalists in several churches represented at the meeting was sharp and instantaneous. They called it an outrageous misrepresentation of the faith and a feminist ploy to undermine the orthodox stances of their churches. Addressing God as "Sophia," said some of them, was blasphemy. The Presbyterian Church, U.S.A., was particularly divided by reactions to the conference. Protests from those who disliked it were vehement, and donations to the denomination's work fell off considerably. Some officials connected with the conference were forced to resign.

As Dr. Patrick Henry, executive director of the Institute for Ecumenical and Cultural Research at Saint John's Abbey and University in Collegeville, Minnesota, and the only male on the planning committee says, "I know, first-hand, the commitment to the church that motivated Re-Imagining. The whole point was *re*-imagining *the tradition,* not inventing something new or reviving old heresies."[37] That is, the participants were not trying to invent a new tradition, but, through their interpretative skills, to breathe new life into the old tradition, the very one all the reactionaries thought they were defending. As Henry goes on to say, "the people in Minneapolis weren't radicals — they were the conservatives, the ones still willing, in spite of the deplorable record of the churches in the treatment of women, in spite of the patriarchalism of the Bible, to stay with the Christian tradition."[38]

Tradition was turned against tradition. The guardians of tradition as the status quo were incensed by the liberties taken by the revisionists, who were only trying to serve their common tradition by refreshing and revitalizing it, by examining it to see which parts were most capable of putting forth green shoots in our present cultural situation. And the same thing happens with great frequency in all institutions: those who truly care about the survival of the tradition and work to achieve its rebirth in new circumstances are attacked by the old guard, who become troubled and defensive if anything about their tradition appears to be even slightly altered.

THIS IS WHAT IS GOING ON in the clamor of conservatives and fundamentalists around the world today. As the noted scholar Karen Armstrong says in *The Battle for God: A History of Fundamentalism*, fundamentalists in virtually every faith in the world have reacted to our rapidly changing global culture by developing a battlefield mentality and displaying a take-no-prisoners attitude toward the defense of their tradition. Ironically, though, their tradition, which they like to think is ancient and venerable, is actually of quite recent origin. The central "fundamental" in all their religions, the literal or plenary inspiration of their Scriptures, was unheard of before the twentieth century.

While the fundamentalists have succeeded in putting religion back at the center of the international agenda, says Armstrong, they have lost sight of "some of the most sacred values of the confessional faiths."

Fundamentalists have turned the *mythos* of their religion into *logos*, either by insisting that their dogmas are scientifically true, or by transforming their complex mythology into a streamlined ideology. They have thus conflated two complementary sources and styles of knowledge which the people in the premodern world had usually decided it was wise to keep separate. The fundamentalist experience shows the truth of this conservative insight. By insisting that the truths of Christianity are factual and scientifically demonstrable, American Protestant fundamentalists have created a caricature of both religion and science. Those Jews and Muslims who have presented their faith in a reasoned, systematic way to compete with other secular ideologies have also distorted their tradition, narrowing it down to a single point by a process of ruthless selection. As a result, all have neglected the more tolerant, inclusive, and compassionate teachings and have cultivated theologies of rage, resentment, and revenge. On occasion, this has even led a small minority to pervert religion by using it to sanction murder. Even the vast majority of fundamentalists, who are opposed to such acts of terror, tend to be exclusive and condemnatory of those who do not share their views.[39]

These words, written before the fanatical Muslim attacks on America on September 11, 2001, were to prove clairvoyant. Their poignancy lies in the way they identify even the fundamentalists' exclusivity and condemnation of others as secondary acts of terrorism. From my own experience, I find the connection tenable. Whether they are encouraging followers to bomb abortion clinics or to infiltrate and disrupt congregations that do not hew exclusively to fundamentalist teachings, conservative and fundamentalist leaders appear to feel little or no moral compunction in terrorizing their opposition.

When I first spoke out against the methods and policies of the Old-Time Gospel Hour in Lynchburg, Virginia, I became an immediate target for attack and elimination by the OTGH's supporters. On more than one occasion, the Rev. Jerry Falwell announced to his OTGH audience, both physically present and via radio (though not on his TV program), "I don't want you to *hurt* Dr. Killinger, but we do not want this man in our town." My family and I were soon receiving death threats, our phone line was tapped, our trash was picked up before the collectors arrived (presumably to be examined), and, according to a U.S. postal inspector, some of our mail was even diverted to someone at the OTGH.

The attacks on my moral character by the California Baptist newspaper following the addresses I gave at Golden Gate Seminary fall under the category of terrorism. So does the threat to boycott Word Books if they did not withdraw my book *For God's Sake, Be Human* from publication. So does the pressure of the religious right on all my publishers to conform to their standards or suffer the consequences in the Christian Booksellers Association market. And the dean of Samford University's Beeson Divinity School's deleting of my name and course offerings from the divinity school computers was an act of terrorism. If I was not as shaken by the events of September 11, 2001, as some of my friends were, it was because I was already well acquainted with the ways of terrorists, albeit not of an extremely violent kind.

WHAT HAPPENED TO ME doesn't really matter. I've been around the block a time or two and I can handle it. But what does matter is the way the fundamentalists terrorize more defenseless people, including their own members. Their whole technique for controlling their situations is to instill as much fear and apprehension in others as possible. This is why their sermons are always so condemnatory and their attitudes so belligerent. They keep everybody on edge by constantly threatening them. They paint God as the Biggest Threat of all — a fiercesome tyrant who targets people for trouble and sends them to hell for not believing and thinking exactly the way the fundamentalists want them to.

Flo Conway and Jim Siegelman discovered this as they did research for their book *Holy Terror: The Fundamentalist War on America's Freedoms in Religion, Politics and Our Private Lives.* Everywhere they went, they found people literally cowering under the threats of fundamentalist teaching. Typical of the people they talked with was a woman named Diane, who lived in a small town in Eastern Pennsylvania. In her midthirties, Diane had gone back to college and met a girl named Sarah Ann in her art class. When she confided to Sarah Ann that life had begun to seem crazy, Sarah Ann began at once trying to convert her, promising that Jesus was the answer to all her problems. Satan was hot on her trail, Sarah Ann warned, and he wouldn't rest until he saw her in hell.

At first it all sounded absurd to Diane. But eventually the dark warnings began to get to her. She went to a prayer meeting with Sarah Ann. It turned out to be a healing service, and Diane was embarrassed by the way people were talking and behaving. On an intellectual level, she rejected everything about the group. But emotionally she was being drawn in. Some of the group members began coming to her house, pressuring her. They would give her Scriptures to read, and some of these made her think that maybe she really was a sinner and needed help.

Slowly, Diane began submitting to the group. They whipsawed her emotionally, shaming her for the evil in her life, then praising her for making progress. When she wouldn't accept Jesus as her Savior, Sarah Ann became angry and broke off their friendship. At first, Diane was mad about this. Then she began to feel rejected and lonely. Her husband, Dan, was impatient with her for being involved with the group and said it was trying to destroy their marriage. This made her even more lonely.

She called up Sarah Ann and asked to see her. Sarah Ann invited her to spend the night at her house. That night, before she went to sleep, Diane invited Jesus into her heart. The next morning, she felt wonderful. Jesus was going to fix everything in her life, she thought.

But the minute she told Sarah Ann and her friends what she had done, they began to take over her life. "They started pulling a lot of new strings," Diane told Conway and Siegelman.

> "They wanted me to conform. Everything that had been important to me now became satanic. I had been active in a local women's group, but they began preaching that the women's movement was satanic. They said you couldn't follow Jesus and be a 'women's libber.' They said that rock music was satanic, which shocked me because I always listened to rock music in the sixties. Then they said that the *sixties* were satanic, that Satan had invaded people in that decade through rock music and sex and drugs. Finally, they began to tell me that certain books were satanic and that we were to go home and look through our bookcases and if we found any books that were not Christian we were to burn them because they were demonic."[40]

The group pressured Diane to witness to others. They began attacking her art, saying that any art that wasn't about Jesus was of the devil. So she gave up her art, along with rock music and her work in the women's movement. Her whole existence seemed to be full of fear and guilt. Everybody in the group was picking at whatever she did or said, saying it wasn't "Christlike." She wondered where the love of God was in their religion. Troubled, she went to the pastor of the church she had joined. He said she asked too many questions. He accused her of being "belligerent" and told her to leave.

Her next few years were a hell. She often felt too sick to
get out of bed and care for her small daughter. Her "friends"
said she was filled with demons. When she was hospitalized,
Sarah Ann called her up and said the whole hospital was full
of demons. "The world was totally ruined to me," said Diane.

> "My Christian friends rejected me, and I was afraid to
> get close to people who weren't born again because
> they were of Satan. After eight years, I tried to read
> a newspaper, but everything seemed to point to Satan
> and the coming destruction of the world. When I tried
> to think, I would get a pain in my head. Things weren't
> connecting. I felt like I had lost my mind. I remembered
> their teaching: 'The mind is the stage of Satan.' I kept
> looking for some little thing that might poke a hole
> in everything I had been taught. I thought, if only I
> could make one little crack in it, I could begin to sort
> it all out."[41]

Fortunately for Diane, something did poke a hole in what
she had been taught. One day she was dusting a bookshelf
and came across an old dictionary with the Declaration of
Independence printed in the back. She read the part about
every person's right to "life, liberty, and the pursuit of happiness." She thought about how little life and liberty she now
enjoyed and how long it had been since she had known
happiness. Suddenly it occurred to her that the Declaration
of Independence was more Christian than her church and
that the U.S. government was more loving and free than
God's government — or at least God's government as she
knew it.

With these thoughts churning in her head, in the spring
of 1980, Diane heard about the "Washington for Jesus"
march. She remembered all the things she had heard from
her Christian friends about Satan's control of our country.
She recalled the itinerant fundamentalist teachers who had

handed out pamphlets about "spiritual dangers" in America and said that a pluralistic society was not acceptable to God. Something inside her snapped. She had to do something. So she went to the march and listened and talked to people. It was exactly as she thought. The fundamentalist leaders were demonizing everything they were opposed to — abortion, the Equal Rights Amendment, and the federal government. The people at the rally were like sheep being led to the slaughter. They didn't even realize their religion had become politicized and was being used to control them. Maybe even to control America.

At last, Diane was on the road to self-recovery. She didn't turn against Jesus. But she knew how Jesus was being used by the fundamentalists, and she refused to be personally terrorized any longer by it. Her long ordeal was over.

Her story, unfortunately, is all too common.

I WON'T TRY to dispute the conservative claim that there is a "liberal establishment" in America and that it controls a lot of old-line media and political centers on the both coasts. Frances Stonor Saunders, in *The Cultural Cold War: The CIA and the World of Arts and Letters,* describes how repeatedly the Old Boy Network sees the scions of WASP families through Groton, Yale, and Harvard Law School, and thence to a Wall Street firm or Fortune 500 company, from which they emerge into undersecretaryships in Washington or positions with the CIA, the FBI, or the IMF.[42] Later, they become members of the boards of various museums, foundations, and major corporations, where they drink cognac with cabinet members and have ready access to the Oval Office. Saunders expresses shock and amazement at this gratuitous intertwining of business, government, academia, and intelligence and shows how the network then affects the attitudes of most important journals, newspapers, and TV companies. They have indeed had a lock on official and semi-official culture-forging for at least the entirety of the twentieth century.

But the paranoiac reaction of the right wing in religious circles is surely not justified by anything the liberal establishment may or may not have done. Freedom of conscience and individual expressions of religious viewpoints have suffered greatly from the duplicity of the conservatives, who pretended to foster liberty at the same time that they were busy undercutting it among any who dared to differ with them.

Jerry Falwell proudly (and ironically) named his school Liberty Baptist College. Larger than it was, it is now Liberty University. Yet it is anything but free. Perry Deane Young, in his book *God's Bullies: Power Politics and Religious Tyranny,* comments: "It seems a sad irony that a school named 'Liberty' operates as a kind of prison, under an extraordinary set of restrictions beginning with this one: 'The college may alter, amend, or abolish its rules or regulations at any time.' "[43] Male students on campus are required to wear ties until after 4:30 p.m. They are not allowed to have beards or mustaches, and their hair must not touch their collars. Female students are forbidden to wear "anything tight, scant, backless, and low in the neckline." Nor may they wear men's pants or jeans at any time. Shorts are off limits to both males and females. Students are to "refrain from listening to rock, disco, country and western, Christian rock, or any other music that is closely associated with these types." They must secure written permission from the dean of students to leave town for the weekend and can be punished or even expelled for dancing, smoking, drinking alcoholic beverages, using profanity, or attending movies.

When I was a pastor in Lynchburg, I was often visited by professors from Liberty Baptist College who needed a friend. One of these professors, Lynn Ridenhour, told me about being stopped on the campus shortly after he arrived and challenged because his hair was too long. Appearing before President Pierre Guillerman, he explained that his ears were badly burned in an automobile fire and the plastic surgeon who reconstructed them advised him to wear a wig that covered the tops of them to avoid getting cancer. Guillerman suggested that Ridenhour trim the wig and wear earmuffs between classes. He refused to do this, saying it would make him the laughing-stock of the campus. After several days of conferring, Guillerman and Falwell agreed that Ridenhour could keep his wig as it was, provided he would carry a letter from his doctor and display it to anyone questioning the length of his hair.

A year or two after joining the Liberty College faculty, Ridenhour was approached by *Penthouse* magazine and asked to write an article describing what it was like to be a faculty member at the infamous institution. He made the mistake of mentioning this project to his best friend on the faculty, and the friend ratted on him to the administration. One afternoon, he was accosted in his office by three men who demanded his notes and anything he had written about the college. He said he didn't know what they were talking about. They refused to leave or to permit him to go. One of them called a friend in the FBI and asked what they should do. Apparently he was told that if they confiscated Ridenhour's typewriter ribbon, it could be used to reconstruct what had been written on it. They removed the ribbon and left.

Ridenhour went to local attorneys, but none of them dared take a case against Falwell on his own turf. Finally, using a Richmond firm, he brought suit against Falwell and the college on the charge of unlawful detention. I could not believe that Falwell would allow the suit to go to court, for it would mean the public disclosure of much embarrassing information. Sure enough, a few days before the suit was slated to be tried, the college settled with Ridenhour for an undisclosed sum of money and the provision that he not talk with reporters.

Ridenhour may have told someone how much he was paid, but he didn't tell me. One thing is certain: he wasn't poor any longer. Several weeks later, he left Lynchburg. He retired from teaching, bought an airplane and three businesses, and took a leisurely trip around the world.

Falwell and other fundamentalist leaders have made skillful use of mass paranoia to rally support from donors who feel weak and vulnerable to the onslaught of change in the modern world. They have constantly decried humanistic forces at work in the world, and have opposed art and literature as instruments of a godless culture. Claiming to be the only true leaders for our time because they are faithful to the letter of the Bible — the *spirit* of the Bible is too elusive for fundamentalists — they set themselves up as judges of everything from sociology to criminology to pop culture, and regularly attack Ivy League schools, Hollywood movies, network television, New York publishers, and anything else that smacks of "establishment."

On August 13, 1981, Falwell sent out an urgent letter to those on his mailing list declaring, "The homosexuals are on the march in this country. Please remember, homosexuals do not reproduce! They recruit! And many of them are out after my children and your children. This is one major reason why we must keep the Old-Time Gospel Hour alive! The Old-Time Gospel Hour is one of the few major ministries in America crying out against militant homosexuals. So don't delay! Let me hear from you immediately! I will be anxiously awaiting your reply."

Terrorism again.

In the spring of 2000, when NBC-TV launched a clever new cartoon program in prime time called *God, the Devil, and Bob,* conservatives attacked the show as irreverent and blasphemous, and Rev. Donald Wildmon's Coalition for Better Television group amassed enough signatures from their computerized mailing list to force NBC to drop it after a few weeks. The show pictured God as a cool dude in sandals and a Hawaiian shirt, and Jim Garner did the marvelous voice overlays for the character. The devil, when he was not impersonating a beautiful woman or some other creature, was a slightly effeminate figure with visible horns. Bob was an auto worker in Detroit who served as a test case for God and Satan: if he learned to love others and live a decent life, God would spare the world for a few more centuries; otherwise he had had it and would please the devil by destroying everything he had created. It was easy to predict that the show would offend conservatives — God often took a beer from the fridge and sometimes used the word "damn." But even if it wasn't as sentimental as *Touched by an Angel*, it was intelligent and often clever, and showed a better understanding of Christian theology than most fundamentalist radio and TV programs.

What gives conservatives the right to dictate to everyone else what they can and can't see on TV and at the movies, or what they can read? Who made them the consciences of the nation? What if liberals fought back and massed together to ban every religious TV show that doesn't meet *their* standards of style and culture? It would wipe out almost every conservative and fundamentalist program on the air! But liberals don't think that way. If they deplore something for its lack of style or intelligence, they usually shrug and go on, figuring it takes all kinds of make a world. Conservatives, on the other hand, want only one kind, *their* kind, and are quick to register their unhappiness with anything that offends them or doesn't conform precisely to their patterns of orthodoxy. They may say they want freedom of expression for everybody, but they are lying through their teeth when they say it.

"YOU WILL KNOW THE TRUTH," said Jesus, "and the truth will make you free" (John 8:32). It is a tantalizing thought, but it is all relative. In this life, we'll never know all the truth. Nor will we ever be completely free.

I didn't realize this when I was a boy growing up in the Baptist church. I assumed that if Jesus said we would know the truth, we would certainly know it. Then I grew up, went to Paris, and had that experience with the Arrabal play at the Thêâtre du Rochechouart. Suddenly I realized how difficult the truth is. How slippery and illusory it is. How it can evaporate in a flash a mere moment after you think you've caught it securely in your own two hands. So freedom is not an easy quest.

What is freedom to me now? Freedom is being comfortable in my own skin. Freedom is not needing the encouragement or approval of someone else to do what I think is right or to believe what I think is true. Freedom is being able to wait with a quiet spirit when I don't understand something or know which way to turn and not be pushed into saying or doing something that is not really me. Freedom is the absence of compulsion. Freedom is being able to write a book like this.

I really identify with the Zen masters who speak of learning to exist happily in nothingness. It is a hard thing to define, but John Leax has come close to it in his memoir, *In Season and Out.* He is speaking of the small orchard on a hillside of his property and how it fits into the scheme of things. It isn't like those endless orchards, with thousands and thousands of trees, that fit into no scheme except maybe the scheme of the market and the desire for profit.

> Perhaps this is why, though I feel my failure to bring the old orchard to fruitfulness, I feel no real guilt, why in fact I feel a sort of pleasure in watching it turn wild and useless. When I walk in it, it tells me that a man's caring comes to an end. It tells me that life is lived within the boundaries of extremes, of wildness and domestication.

It tells me that my order is not the only order. And in its message I find comfort.[44]

That's the same message I got that day from the play by Arrabal, and the feeling that what went on in that crazy theater was more real than what was going on when I came out into the quiet back streets of Paris: "my order is not the only order."

There's a strange comfort in that. I wouldn't have known it years ago, but it's good not to be in charge of things, and not to want to be in charge. There is a kind of freedom in not feeling that you are responsible for what happens — that God is perfectly capable of taking care of the world in his own time and in his own way, and I don't need to rush about, reordering it to suit my limited notion of what he would like. I don't even mind that fundamentalists think the way they do. I just don't want them telling me how I have to think and what I have to believe. Or anybody else, for that matter. I want everybody to be as free as I am, and it ticks me off for them to act as if God gave them the supervisory contract on the world.

I never feel freer than I do when I'm walking the hills of the Lake District, in England, or soaking in my bathtub at home. In neither place is there any compulsion for me to do anything or make any kind of statement. And in both places I feel exceptionally close to God — cradled in divine grace, caught up in timeless wonder. There, I don't have to *do* anything to please God. I don't have to think or believe anything in particular. I am simply there, and he is there, and it is enough.

As I said in the beginning of this book, I am grateful to the church I grew up in for introducing me to God. But I have learned a lot about him since then — and a lot about myself. We are both very different from who we were then, or who I thought we were. I am very comfortable with God, and trust that he is comfortable with me. Like old friends, we have come a long way together.

All the things I've talked about in this book — the ten wrong teachings — were at one time an important part of my life and thought. But not anymore. And I don't think God minds that I've given them up. They turned out to be a lot less important than I thought they were. In fact, some of them turned out to be real bummers. Now, I feel free, not because I have learned all the truth, but because I don't need to learn it all. Because I have learned enough of it to know which things are truly meaningful to me at this present moment, and which are not.

I like what Alfred North Whitehead, the brilliant mathematician and philosopher, said in one of his lectures on "Religion in History." It really brings everything together — truth, freedom, and God.

> The religious insight is the grasp of this truth: That the order of the world, the depth of reality of the world, the value of the world in its whole and in its parts, the beauty of the world, the zest for life, the peace of life, and the mastery of evil, are all bound together — not accidentally, but by reason of this truth: that the universe exhibits a creativity with infinite freedom, and a realm of forms with infinite possibilities; but that this creativity and these forms are together impotent to achieve actuality apart from the completed ideal harmony, which is God.[45]

Of all the sweet-spirited conservatives I have known in the course of my life, one of the finest was Stanley Mooneyham. Stan had been a Baptist minister in Mississippi and eventually became president of World Vision and a special assistant to Billy Graham. He traveled the world for Christ and knew almost everybody who was anybody in conservative circles. Then, in his midfifties, Stan and his wife divorced and he was dropped like a hot potato. All his conservative friends acted as if he had leprosy.

Regathering himself, Stan started earning his living as a consultant, got married again, and renegotiated his life. I met him when I was a pastor in Los Angeles and he and his new wife would sometimes drive in for church from their home in Palm Desert. Occasionally I invited Stan to have the morning prayer in the service. It was always an experience to hear him pray. He had a way of carrying everybody right up to the throne of grace and then having a picnic there.

In 1989, Stan published a book called *Dancing on the Strait and Narrow: A Gentle Call to a Radical Faith.* It was his statement of faith to all the people who had known and deserted him when their religion wouldn't let them be friends with him anymore. He said in the preface to the book, "I owe a great debt to the religious systems of which I am a product, but I am also suspicious of them because they are still preoccupied with the shape of the loaf rather than the quality of the bread."[46]

He understood, he said, that insistence on conformity is an effective means of self-preservation for conservative believers, and that mavericks are too threatening to a wellordered system. Yet he said he believed the system "loses a great deal in the long run by forcing out or freezing out the independent inquirers."[47]

Stan talked in the book about the legalistic and repressive system under which he grew up and how it dogged him most of his adult life, making him constricted and fearful. He caught glimpses of Jesus as a dancer but couldn't bring himself to join the dance. It was easier and safer to go along with his conservative friends, subscribing to their ethics and taking swipes at people who seemed to be having more fun. Then, one day in midlife, he decided to stop reinventing himself all the time in the images of his friends and who they wanted him to be. He began an inner search for the person he thought God wanted him to be. Eventually he was able to stand up to his friends with their high-control needs and say who he really was and what he wanted to be in the kingdom of God. By the time he wrote the book, he could say emphatically that he liked the real person he was better than the public images he had spent so much of his energy trying to maintain.

Did he have any advice for his old friends in the conservative and fundamentalist camps? Yes, he did. That advice was to "make friends with your shadow." It was to stop trying to rule everybody's life and make it conform to a legalistic pattern, and to learn to live in peace with the darker sides of their own nature. Then perhaps even they too would transcend their fear of dancing and join the Lord of the dance.

I wish it were possible. Then we would all be free.

Afterword

Reviewing this book, I realize how fitting it is that I began with the chapter on the Bible. If I had remained a biblical literalist, believing that every word in the Bible was somehow either mystically or actually dictated by God, I would never have become free enough of my fundamentalist upbringing to reach the set of beliefs and attitudes that presently determine who I am. I would have remained a part of the "no-brainer" religion described by Mark Noll in *The Scandal of the Evangelical Mind.*

Taken too zealously, the Bible severely delimits our ability to grow beyond its ancient worldview. It describes a whimsical deity who created woman from a man's rib, indenturing her forever to the male gender and forbidding her to become a leader or teacher of men. It pictures a legalistic society where people can be killed for uttering blasphemies, dishonoring their parents, or simply being homosexual. It glorifies holy wars waged in the deity's name, and even justifies genocide. It lustily envisions the horrible deaths of religious outsiders in lakes of eternal fire.

I have a profound respect for the Bible and the higher spirit encountered in its loftier passages. As a preacher, I have always taken seriously the importance of the biblical text as a basis for my sermons, trying to "speak where the Bible speaks and remain silent where it is silent." It is, after all, the one collection of writings agreed upon as Christendom's central authority — more for Protestants, of course, than for Roman Catholics — and remains as such our overriding family document. And so many of its nobler verses are stored in my memory that no day passes without my unconscious mind feeding on them and nudging some of them into consciousness, where they prove apt and relevant commentary on the world around me.

But I am quite satisfied, after years of dealing with the question of the Bible's authority, that God never intended it to become the restrictive document it has become in the hands of the fundamentalists. There are many wonderful things in its pages, but it is only a passing record of humanity's experience of the Holy over a period of a few thousand years, and a somewhat limited record at that, considering the vast literatures of ancient Egypt, Greece, India, and China. Any God whose parameters are defined by the Bible alone is too small for the yearnings and understandings of the twenty-first-century heart.

The filmmakers of *The Gods Must Be Crazy,* in which an African tribe idolizes and worships a Coke bottle that falls out of an airplane passing overhead, understood better than most conservatives and fundamentalists the anthropological dimensions of religious artifacts. Whenever we idolize the Scriptures, turning them into monuments of infallible truth and wisdom, we are little better than the worshipers of the Coke bottle, for we attribute to the book itself *mana* or powers it cannot possibly possess.

Jerry Falwell was right, back in chapter one, about the slippery slope. Once we are able to say out loud that the Bible is not the inerrant word of God — that its inspiration is not really different from that of the Bhagavad-Gita or Thoreau's *Walden* or Maya Angelou's poems — then a great number of conservative and fundamentalist idols begin to topple. It is from thence a simple step to denying that Jesus is the only way to God or that he really had to die for our sins. And it takes but a little imagination to see that the church is not actually in charge of the world's salvation after all, and cannot say who is and who isn't going to enter the kingdom of God.

The truth is, Christians today ought to be *better* than most of our forebears in the early Scriptures ever thought of being, for we are the heirs of whole libraries of musings about how we ought to think and be in light of ancient Judaism's first-century encounter with Jesus of Nazareth. We ought to aspire to higher goals of godliness and humanity and establish institutions freer of prejudice and anthropomorphic ideologies. We ought to understand enough about education to raise whole generations of truly sympathetic and enlightened followers who will manage better than the people of any previous era to turn the kingdoms of this world into the kingdom of our Christ.

Instead, we content ourselves with reproducing in every age the narrowness of mind and limitations of vision that afflicted the generation before, and delude ourselves into believing that all God wants or requires of any of us is a simple adulation of the book and the practices that have marked our religion from its inception. We are as slavish in our repetition of the past as the heirs of some old Southern dynasty, unwilling for time to move forward or once-cherished ideals to give way to new ones.

THE APRIL 16, 2000, issue of *The Washington Post Magazine* carried a long account by Martha Sherrill of "The Buddha from Poolesville," a woman named Jetsunma, who in the suburbs of Maryland has built the largest Tibetan Buddhist monastery in the U.S. Until 1986, Jetsunma was Alyce Zeoli, a young woman who grew up in Brooklyn, had three marriages, and struggled most of her life with a weight problem. Then she met His Holiness Penor Rinpoche, a man so venerable that people in India save the clods of dirt he walks on. Rinpoche took one look at Jetsunma and announced that she was a "great great *bodhisattva* of many lifetimes" — the *tulku,* or reincarnation, of great Buddhist saints — and her whole life changed. Suddenly she was revered by thousands of people, and her remarkable odyssey as Jetsunma began.

In the course of the interview she did for the *Post,* Sherrill interviewed Jetsunma several times. On one occasion they talked about Jetsunma's adopted daughter, Atira. Jetsunma said that Atira was the daughter of a drug-addicted girl named Jalee, who had come to the monastery for help. In the fall of 1987, Jalee told Jetsunma she was pregnant. They discussed what could be done. Jetsunma recalled that Jalee had considered abortion, but Jetsunma had talked her out of it and had brought her a list of possible adoptive parents. Jetsunma's name was on the list, though she didn't relish the thought of taking the child.

WHEN THE CHILD WAS BORN and Jetsunma saw her, she recognized the baby as her own daughter and insisted that she be the one to adopt her. She even gave an "executive order" that she be the one to take the child.

Jalee eventually became a Buddhist nun and assumed the new name of Catherine Anastasia. Sherrill interviewed her, too. Jalee, or Catherine, did not remember the story as Jetsunma did. In fact, she said she had not even considered abortion as a possibility. She came to Jetsunma, she said, to ask whether she should keep the child herself or put it up for adoption.

Sherrill pounced on this inconsistency. How could Jalee, or Catherine, reconcile herself with this misunderstanding and continue to serve under Jetsunma? "I just do," said the nun. "There is really only one version of this story. Whatever Jetsunma told you is the real version. Whatever I remember is just my experience, and only my experience."

I laid the magazine aside when I read this and pondered Jalee's words. *Whatever Jetsunma had told was the real version.* Whatever Jalee remembered was only her experience and not the truth.

I thought about this book and how outspoken I have been in rejecting my conservative background. Something inside me, some small part of my self, wanted to repeat what Jalee had said and to denounce the places where I diverge from my background as "only my experience" and not really the truth. How comforting that would be, I thought — to put it all down to the dyspepsia of my latter years and somehow preserve a loyalty to the simple faith of my childhood.

But I cannot do it, any more than Martin Luther could renounce what he had personally experienced in favor of the understanding of the Church of Rome. My experience is important. If I renounce it, I nullify my whole pilgrimage. Even worse, I say that no one's experience is worth a second thought compared to the teachings of that person's mother church, the background from which he or she emerged. There might as well not have been a Protestant revolution. We could all simply return to the Holy Roman Church — the one before Vatican II — and embrace all the superstitions of the Middle Ages.

I cannot and will not say that everything in this book is right for anyone but myself. But I do claim it as my experience and insist that it is not rendered worthless by being "only my experience." And I also insist that every individual ought to make his or her own pilgrimage of faith — like Sir Francis Chichester steering the *Gypsy Moth* toward the most recent sundogs he spotted on his way to Australia — and be willing to live by the consequences. Only that, it seems to me, is real faith and real freedom. All the rest is pseudofaith, an imitation of the real thing. Kierkegaard was right to insist that he have no followers, because in spiritual matters each person must make his or her own way.

As Whitehead said, "Religion is what the individual does with his own solitariness.... If you are never solitary, you are never religious. Collective enthusiasms, revivals, institutions, churches, rituals, bibles, codes of behaviour, are the trappings of religion, its passing forms."[48]

THE ONE THING for which I shall remain eternally grateful to my conservative upbringing is its strong insistence on the grace of God. Although I grew up in a home where I sometimes had reason not to trust my parents, even though I loved them devotedly, I learned implicitly to trust my heavenly Father. There has never been a moment in my entire life as a Christian when I have had the least doubt of God's love for me or his infinite care about what happens to me.

It is this trust that has permitted me to experiment with my faith, to be like a high-wire artist working out new and challenging routines, knowing there is always a safety net below, that however outrageously mistaken I may be, or however clumsy, I cannot in the end commit a fatal blunder. God's arms are always there. They were there before I even learned of him, and they will be there when I die.

In chapters three and eight, I mentioned the vision I had of the angel Gabriel. One day in my midlife, when I was feeling the extreme pressure of making a change to another home and workplace — I could almost call it a panic — I had a dream. Actually, it was a waking dream, which occurred while I was meditating. I was on the Mediterranean island of Paros, staying in a hotel our son Eric and I had once visited on a backpacking trip through the Greek Isles. The hotel sat on a little hill overlooking the picture-postcard harbor. I saw a commotion below as a ship sailed into the harbor, and I ran down to join it. The ship was a Spanish galleon, and the captain who descended the gangplank, once it was secured to the dock, wore a plumed helmet. He looked like the figure in Rembrandt's painting *The Man in a Golden Helmet*. As he reached the dock, he and I stood face to face. He removed the helmet and I beheld the gaunt, luminous visage I had seen so many years earlier. It was the angel Gabriel.

"Don't you realize," he said, "I have always been with you."

It was a very comforting thought at a particularly difficult time of my life. I have not forgotten it and never will. He has always been with me. I cannot sail beyond his care or fall beneath his protection. God's provision is more than ample and can never be exhausted, wherever I go or whatever I do.

Ironically, it seems to me, this is what the conservative church never appears to realize. It *talks* about the unfailing grace of God, but it has never been able to *practice* it. All my conservative and fundamentalist friends — perhaps they would be more comfortable if I only called them "acquaintances" — seem to have a kind of provisionality about their faith. God will save them, *provided.*... God will love them, *provided.*... They will be good Christians, *provided.*...

I am grateful to God for a nature that has never worried about such provisions. I know I am a sinful creature, and that my vision is imperfect and my understanding incomplete. But I also know, in the very depths of my heart, that God can be trusted and that my imperfections do not really matter to him. God's love is too great for such finicky concerns. It simply overwhelms everything, the way the love of the father did in Jesus' story of the Prodigal Son, when he wouldn't even listen to his son's confession but smothered him in kisses and embraces.

When our older son was about two years old, I dedicated a book to him and said in the dedication, "I understand God better now that we are both fathers." That wasn't a flippant remark. It was a serious theological comment. When I had children and realized how boundless my love for them is, so that no crime they could ever commit against nature would exclude them from my heart, I knew I understood in a small way the indescribable love and grace of my heavenly Father, who only smiles at my peccadilloes and looks with parental favor on my eccentricities.

It is the assurance of this divine love, "all loves excelling," that has permitted — even encouraged — my wandering from the path of my church's teachings and my delight in the way of a seeker. All God's children who know anything of his grace should become seekers, willing to follow the road less taken in order to discover the marvels of hidden grottoes and the extraordinary flowers on the craggiest heights. Most of the memorable characters in Christian history, beginning with Jesus himself, have been seekers. They have refused to say, like Jalee, "There is only one story, and it is the real one. My version is only my experience and is therefore not real."

The only real story, seekers know, is the one they *own* as real, the one to which they can put their signatures because they have lived it and felt it and pushed its envelope to the limits. To them, everything else is false. Not because it is intrinsically false, but because it hasn't been lived. Only what they can actually experience is true. Everything else is subreal.

Now, as I reflect on my life and the things I've written in this book, I am filled with a sense of deep peace. And I would be pleased and honored if it could be said of me, as Annie-Laurie in Elizabeth Goudge's novel *Pilgrim's Inn* says of the country parson, Hilary Eliot: "One felt that whatever his past troubles he had come through them. He had the peacefulness of a ship drawing near to the harbor, and entering it gently with slight headway on."[49]

Notes

1. Frederick Buechner, *The Alphabet of Grace* (New York: Seabury Press, 1970), 3–4.

2. W. A. Criswell, *Why I Preach That the Bible Is Literally True* (Nashville: Broadman Press, 1969), 46.

3. Ibid., 79.

4. Walter Harrelson, "Passing on the Biblical Tradition Intact: The Role of Historical Criticism," in *Beyond the Impasse? Scripture, Interpretation, and Theology in Baptist Life,* ed. Robison B. James and David S. Dockery (Nashville: Broadman Press, 1992), 40–41.

5. John Shelby Spong, *Rescuing the Bible from Fundamentalism: A Bishop Rethinks the Meaning of Scripture* (New York: HarperCollins, 1991), 14–15.

6. Robert W. Funk, *Honest to Jesus: Jesus for a New Millennium* (San Francisco: HarperSanFrancisco, 1966), 42.

7. Edna St. Vincent Millay, "God's World," in *Modern American Poetry,* ed. Louis Untermeyer (New York: Harcourt, Brace and Company, 1950), 462.

8. Herschel H. Hobbs, *The Baptist Faith and Message* (Nashville: Convention Press, 1971), 36.

9. Robert Bolt, *A Man for All Seasons* (New York: Vintage, 1990), 162.

10. Cited by David J. Bromell in "Processing towards Death," a lecture at the first Australasian Conference on Process Philosophy and Process Theology, "The Contemporary Relevance of Process Thought," Sydney, Australia, May 23–25, 1997. Bromell also cites this passage from Whitehead: "The consequent nature of God is his judgment on the world. He saves the world as it passes into the immediacy of his own life. It is the judgment of a tenderness which loses nothing that can be saved. It is also the judgment of a wisdom which uses what in the temporal world is mere wreckage."

11. E. Stanley Jones, *Christ at the Round Table* (London: Hodder & Stoughton, 1928), 10–11.

12. Ibid., 287.

13. Bruce Bower, *Stealing Jesus: How Fundamentalism Betrays Christianity* (New York: Crown Publishers, 1997), 5–7, 244–46.

14. John A. T. Robinson, *But That I Can't Believe!* (London: Collins/Fontana, 1967), 127.

15. Dean M. Kelley, *Why Conservative Churches Are Growing* (New York: Harper & Row, 1972), 88–90.

16. Rubem Alves, *Tomorrow's Child* (New York: Harper & Row, 1972), 112.

17. Marcus Borg, *Meeting Jesus Again for the First Time* (San Francisco: HarperSanFrancisco, 1994), 32.

18. Jimmy Allen, *Burden of a Secret* (New York: Ballantine Books, 1995).

19. Janwillem van de Wetering, *A Glimpse of Nothingness* (New York: Ballantine Books, 1975), 51–52.

20. Ibid., 179.

21. H. A. Williams, *Some Day I'll Find You* (London: Collins Fount Paperbacks, 1984), 247.

22. Frederick Buechner, *The Sacred Journey* (San Francisco: Harper & Row, 1982), 3.

23. Charlene Kaemmerling, "Ordination of Women: Right or Wrong?" *Theological Educator* (Spring 1988): 99.

24. Bailey Smith, cited by Bill Leonard in *God's Last and Only Hope: The Fragmentation of the Southern Baptist Convention* (Grand Rapids: William B. Eerdmans, 1990), 153.

25. Jerry Falwell, cited by William R. Goodman, Jr., and James J. H. Price, eds., *Jerry Falwell: An Unauthorized Profile* (Lynchburg, Va.: Paris & Associates, 1981), 129.

26. Mark Noll, *The Scandal of the Evangelical Mind* (Grand Rapids: William B. Eerdmans, 1994), 137.

27. Dan Wakefield, *How Do We Know When It's God?* (New York: Little, Brown and Company, 1999), 114–15.

28. John Updike, *Roger's Version* (New York: Alfred A. Knopf, 1986), 10.

29. Allen, *Burden*, 152.

30. Archibald MacLeish, *J.B.: A Play in Verse* (New York: Houghton Mifflin, 1961), 89.

31. Harold Kushner, *When Bad Things Happen to Good People* (New York: Schocken Books, 1981), 85.

32. Ibid., 113–14.

33. Ibid., 115.

34. David Steindl-Rast, *Gratefulness, the Heart of Prayer* (Ramsey, N.J.: Paulist Press, 1984), 11.

35. Glenn Hinson, in *The Struggle for the Soul of the SBC*, ed. Walter B. Shurden (Macon, Ga.: Mercer University Press, 1993), 15.

36. Ibid.

37. Patrick Henry, *The Ironic Christian's Companion: Finding the Marks of God's Grace in the World* (New York: Riverhead Books, 1999), 160.

38. Ibid., 161–62.

39. Karen Armstrong, *The Battle for God: A History of Fundamentalism* (New York: Ballantine Books, 2001), 366.

40. Flo Conway and Jim Siegelman, *Holy Terror: The Fundamentalist War on America's Freedoms in Religion, Politics and Our Private Lives* (New York: Doubleday, 1982), 18.

41. Ibid., 23.

42. New York: The New Press, 2000.

43. Perry Deane Young, *God's Bullies: Power Politics and Religious Tyranny* (New York: Holt, Rinehart & Winston, 1982), 214.

44. John Leax, *In Season and Out* (Grand Rapids: Zondervan, 1985), 31.

45. Alfred North Whitehead, "Body and Spirit," a lecture given in his "Religion and History" series at King's Chapel, Boston, February 1926.

46. W. Stanley Mooneyham, *Dancing On the Strait and Narrow: A Gentle Call to Radical Faith* (San Francisco: Harper & Row, 1989), ix.

47. Ibid.

48. Whitehead, "Body and Spirit."

49. Elizabeth Goudge, *Pilgrim's Inn* (New York: Coward-McCann, 1948), 230.

About the Author

JOHN KILLINGER has had a distinguished career as church-man, professor, and author. Holder of a Ph.D. in theology from Princeton and another in literature from the University of Kentucky, he taught preaching, worship, and literature at Vanderbilt Divinity School from 1965 to 1980. He has also taught as a visiting professor at the University of Chicago, City College of New York, Princeton Seminary, and Clare-mont School of Theology, and was Distinguished Professor of Religion and Culture at Samford University in Birmingham.

Ordained as a Baptist minister at the age of eighteen, he left teaching for a decade in the 1980s to be senior minister of the First Presbyterian Church in Lynchburg, Virginia, where he clashed with Lynchburg's most famous citizen, Rev. Jerry Falwell, and then became senior minister of the First Congregational Church of Los Angeles, the oldest English-speaking congregation in that city. Since leaving Samford University in 1996, he has been minister of the Little Stone Church on Mackinac Island, Michigan, a resort church visited annually by thousands of people from all over the world.

He has written more than fifty books, on subjects ranging from Hemingway and the Theater of the Absurd to prayer, preaching, and biblical commentary. He has also served on the editorial boards of *Christian Ministry, Pulpit Digest,* and the Library of Distinctive Sermons.

Killinger and his wife, Anne, love reading, writing, travel, theater, and hiking. Their rambling home is on the outskirts of Warrenton, Virginia, halfway between the nation's capital and the Blue Ridge Mountains.

Index

OF RELATED INTEREST

Kim Jocelyn Dickson
GIFTS FROM THE SPIRIT
Reflections on the Diaries and Letters
of Anne Morrow Lindbergh

In *Gifts from the Spirit,* Dickson tells how her own life has been transformed by Anne Morrow Lindbergh's writings. Drawing from Lindbergh's diaries, and including her own evocative reflections, Dickson captures the essence of Lindbergh's spirituality and womanhood.

0-8245-2010-6, $17.95 hardcover

Brennan Manning
THE JOURNEY OF THE PRODIGAL
A Parable of Growth and Redemption

In *The Boy Who Cried Abba,* Brennan Manning introduced readers to Willie Juan — an orphaned boy who meets Jesus and learns the value of unconditional love. In this sequel, Willie Juan has become an adult and, as he struggles with alcoholism and depression, discovers that he has to relearn the lessons of his childhood. His story is a modern parable for our own search for wholeness and unconditional love.

0-8245-2014-9, $14.95 paperback

Paula D'Arcy
A NEW SET OF EYES
Encountering the Hidden God

Through a series of meditations and parables, D'Arcy helps readers awaken the mind to the presence of God, free the soul from its cherished idols, and infuse the emotions with joy. By the popular author of *Gift of the Red Bird* and *Song for Sarah.*

0-8245-1930-2, $16.95 hardcover

crossroad

OF RELATED INTEREST

Barbara Fiand
IN THE STILLNESS YOU WILL KNOW
Exploring the Paths of Our Ancient Belonging

Popular spirituality writer Barbara Fiand is back with a moving book inspired by death of her dearest friend and soulmate. Shadowed by grief, Fiand uses her friend's untimely passing as the starting point for ponderings about the nature of hope and the solace that comes from the beauty of nature speaking to us.

0-8245-2650-3, $16.95 paperback

Michael Morwood
GOD IS NEAR
Trusting Our Faith

In his latest book, the author of *Tomorrow's Catholic* and *Is God Jesus God?* reminds readers that the Christian God is closer to us than our very hearts. He seeks to counter commonly held notions — like the need for people to earn or be worthy of God's love — with the loving portrait of the Father handed down by Jesus and captured in the Gospels.

0-8245-1984-1, $12.95 paperback

Please support your local bookstore,
or call 1-800-707-0670 for Customer Service.

For a free catalog, write us at

THE CROSSROAD PUBLISHING COMPANY
481 Eighth Avenue, Suite 1550
New York, NY 10001

Visit our website at
www.crossroadpublishing.com

crossroad